MYTHS AND MADNESS

By

Miriam Kove

ISBN: 1-4107-0869-1 (e-book)
ISBN: 1-4107-0870-5 (Paperback)

Library of Congress Control Number: 2003090653

This book is printed on acid free paper.

Printed in the United States of America
Bloomington, IN

1stBooks - rev. 08/14/03

Take stock of those around you and you will hear them talk in precise terms about themselves and their surroundings, which would seem to point to their having ideas about the matter. But start to analyze these ideas and you will find that they hardly reflect in any way the reality to which they appear to refer, and if you go deeper you will discover that there is not even an attempt to adjust the ideas to this reality. Quite the contrary: through these notions the individual is trying to cut off any personal vision of reality, of his own very life. For life is at the start a chaos in which one is lost. The individual suspects this, but he is frightened at finding himself face to face with this terrible reality, and tries to cover it over with a curtain of fantasy, where everything is clear. It does not worry him that his "ideas" are not true, he uses them as trenches for the defense of his existence, as scarecrows to frighten away reality.

José Ortega Y Gasset
The Revolt of the Masses

Neurosis in a nutshell-the miscarriage of clumsy lies about reality.

To my daughters
who are sometimes myth, sometimes madness—
but always joy!

She was 13 years old with large, dark eyes that looked with surprised sadness at the world. After 4 years of therapy, she had finally whispered to me her central secret. She was "magic." She could make things happen just by wishing them or wanting them. Last summer, she had caused a boy in camp, whom she hated, to break his arm.

Her large eyes filled with tears. "He deserved it. He was always making me strike out at baseball. Let him feel what it was like to be awkward. God will understand." On and on it went, each sentence making more clear the pain that this child was suffering, the conflict, the ambivalence between seeing herself as a superior being—a grandiose magic goddess—and the terror she felt at having and using such power.

Days and weeks later, after much exploration of details and incidents that "attested" to this magic power, and exploration of her glee and pain and guilt and shame, she was able to tell of the experience that convinced her of her specialness. She was 3 years old. She was stuck, with her family, in a traffic jam. It was hot in the car. The family was on the way to a wedding. They were going to be late. Clothes were wilting and tempers were flaring. Diane, my patient, was crying.

"Diane," said her mother. "Tell those cars to move."

"Move, cars," said Diane. At that moment, the cars started to move. Diane's mother hugged her and said, "You did it!"

Perhaps the mother was playing. The child was not. At three years old, her understanding was literal. When her mother said that she could make things happen by words and wishes, Diane believed her. Thus was the unconscious concept of magical thinking confirmed in the child's psyche by a coincidental mother's word.

Lila was 65 when she came to see me; a grey-haired, mature, very handsome lady. She had had a very productive life: a career, a good marriage, an affectionate relationship with her grown-up children, friends and interesting activities. She was presenting herself in therapy because she had recently almost died from a bleeding ulcer. Her doctor suggested that she seek help to better understand and manage her stress.

Lila began to talk haltingly about her brother, with whom she had once been very close. He had literally abandoned her, not inviting her to his silver anniversary, and not coming to see her in the hospital when she was "at death's door." He had not been there for her to lean on when her husband had died.

Lila's brother had not shared with her why he was doing this. Lila felt lost, full of pain and confusion. Gently, I suggested that she probably felt some anger at being abandoned by someone she had loved and counted on so heavily. She looked at me in great astonishment, saying, "Of course I'm not angry! I love my brother!"

A year later, when Lila could feel and express some of her rage at her brother, she also felt ashamed and afraid. "It's bad to feel anger," she confided in me. "A good person loves, only loves."

Apparently, that was the message that Lilia had received from her mother in her youth. Whenever her bombastic father let loose his violent temper, leaving the children cowering in the corner, her mother would say, "It's OK. People in a family love each other."

When Lila complained bitterly that her sister had left her with all the dishes to wash, and it was not her turn, her mother would say, "You have to help your sister. People in a family love each other."

Lila absorbed and outwardly accepted this message. No matter how much denial, avoidance, rationalization and repression were necessary, they were to be preferred to anger, resentment and revenge. Only love was allowed in the family vocabulary. No one ever told Lila that anger pushed aside sometimes stormed back as a bleeding ulcer.

Of course, behavior, symptoms, patterns and fantasies are multi-determined. Various events and occurrences cluster around a central idea or experience to form a belief system. The strands that lead to a held idea or pattern or behavior are complex, varied and meandering.

For instance, a person who overeats may do so for many reasons. He may overeat because he is afraid of sex and wants to make himself unattractive, as a means of avoiding it. He may overeat because unconsciously, he feels like an abandoned baby at peril of starvation. He may do so because, on some level, he feels worthless and bad, and needs to punish himself for his "badness" by self-destructive behavior. He may view slimness as power, power that he didn't work for, doesn't deserve, and should negate.

Sometimes overeating stems from an attempt to maintain a connection with a parent-usually, a parent who would prefer his child to be thin. By overeating, the child can remain connected, yet gives himself the illusion of separation by adolescent rebellious behavior. In other words, the child is pursuing a behavior that is antithetical to the parent's wish and this makes him feel "grown up" but, because it's not an autonomous choice related to what he wants but rather is related to what the parent doesn't want, the argument and connection continue.

An individual may share some or all of these reasons for overeating, or more, in different and various quality and quantity. To understand and unearth their strands and history is detailed and complicated work. I wish to focus on just one of these strands, an important one that affects our belief system about who we are as people, what the world is, and how we behave with ourselves and in the world.

In brief, our culture and society promote certain ideas—both spoken and unspoken. These ideas are handed down from generation to generation, and accepted as true when they are false. The myths I refer to cause discomfort, pain, confusion, non-productive behavior and, yes, even madness in our world.

One such idea, to which I alluded earlier, consists of the belief that anger and negative feelings are "wrong," "bad" or "naughty." Many of my patients have been taught that they are "wrong" or "bad" to feel negative feelings of any kind, including disappointment, sadness, grief, guilt and fear. They also feel that they should neither acknowledge nor discuss these feelings, when they do arise.

A patient with a 3 year old daughter brought me the following tale. She was a concerned and loving mother and wanted very much to help her daughter grow into a healthy adult. My patient and her daughter had been in the park, walking among the fall leaves and sliding down fire engine slides, when the little girl noticed an animal on the ground. Approaching it carefully, she looked it over.

"Mommy," she said, starting to cry, "the squirrel is dead!" To which her mother, wanting no trauma for the child, replied, "No, honey, he is only sleeping."

Her child looked up at her in disbelief and said nothing. Thus, the loving mother had inadvertently lied to her daughter and tampered with her daughter's sense and understanding of reality. She had also taken away from her child a chance to confront death, an important fact of existence, and to grieve for the dying of a living being. Through her mother's dismissal and denial of the reality of the situation, the child received the message that death and loss and pain and sadness were "bad" feelings, to be avoided at all costs.

Most of us, at some point, have heard the expression "Big boys don't cry." Why don't they cry? They feel pain, sadness, disappointment and frustration, just like the rest of us. The suggestion in "big boys don't cry" is that crying is weak, and that "real" men should be stoic and expressionless. This philosophy often results in producing men who are cut off from their ability to feel or show feelings.

When President Kennedy died and a nation was devastated with grief, we admired Jacqueline Kennedy and her children as they followed the coffin, tearless and outwardly calm. John John pathetically saluted his father's coffin as it passed.

We hailed the family as "brave" and hallelujahed Jacqueline's stance and posture. As a nation, we embraced the idea and theatre of death and loss without feeling. Yet how much "braver" and better it would have been for the Kennedys to weep and wail; to act as the Irish do in Sean O'Casey plays; to display grief at the loss of a beloved son, husband and father; to raise their fists to Heaven in anger that this man was taken from them in the bloom of life and accomplishment. How much better to reveal to an attentive nation the feelings that such a tragedy arouses; how much better to mourn healthily and wholeheartedly, rather than feed the national myth that one should endure painful circumstances without feeling or showing pain.

Several years ago, I attended a lecture in my daughter's school. The topic of the lecture was *Parenting Without Guilt* and the talk was given by a PhD psychologist. Her thesis was that parents need not feel any guilt about the manner and style of raising their children, that each parent had a right to parent in his fashion and according to his wishes and that to feel guilt about a particular practice or outcome was to be "wrong." Guilt as a feeling and a word was to be eliminated from the parent's linguistic and emotional vocabulary.

Various parents raised their hands. One woman felt guilty because, as a child, she had been afraid of rollerskating and hence did not allow her child to rollerskate with his friends. One man felt guilty because his child had asked to take a writing class with a man who was a warm, kind, caring teacher. Fearing that the teacher was homosexual, the father had denied his child's request. Another mother felt guilty because she pushed food on her overweight child and could not seem to stop.

The psychologist absolved them, one and all. "As parents," she said, "You have a right to parenting without guilt. Relax and keep doing whatever you're doing."

I saw and listened in dumb disbelief. I thought that here was a person who had been made to feel terribly guilty as a child and wanted to eradicate the idea of guilt so that she could feel worthwhile. Or else she had been told as a child that guilt was "bad," and needed to be pushed away. So now she was trying to push it away with all her might. In the service of that (given her education), she was expounding a theory that she must have known to be terribly non-productive, hurtful and misleading.

Not to feel appropriately guilty when one is doing something wrong is to have no conscience, to be psychopathic; it is to inflict harm on others as if you have all rights and they have none; it is to have no control against mayhem and anarchy.

Guilt is a precious feeling. When appropriate, it guides us to loving, caring action and behavior towards others. When inappropriate, it can be damaging to ourselves and to others.

What we need to do is not abolish guilt but examine it when it occurs and consider its appropriateness. The three parents described above all felt appropriately guilty. Each, in his own fashion, was using his own feelings and prejudices to act out on his children. They were denying their children that to which they had a right and which was good for them. The guilt was a signal to the parent that something was wrong, that they needed to investigate their behavior for the welfare of their offspring. Instead, the therapist gave them carte blanche to override their guilty feelings.

At this point, the reader may wonder what is so important. What's the big deal? What happens when one denies and submerges negative feelings?

One of the things that happens is that since we deny that we have these feelings, we don't learn to deal with them productively. If a man acknowledges to himself that he feels angry with his wife, he can then attempt to understand what is causing this anger. Perhaps she is spending all her time with the children, leaving him feeling unattended to and lonely. If he can express these feelings to his wife, they may find ways to solve the problem.

But if he is unaware of his rage, because he has been trained to avoid "bad" feelings, he will neither feel nor express it openly. Instead he will act out. He may forget her birthday, take a mistress, become impotent, etc.

Negative feelings do not go away. If not recognized, accepted and dealt with, they go temporarily underground. Then they emerge in headaches, ulcers, asthma, perhaps cancer, nightmares, suicide, alcoholism, drug addiction, adolescent runaways, eating disorders, obsessive-compulsive behavior, destructive patterns, etc.

It is my contention that at least one strand of the formation of these disorders stems from anger and pain left unexpressed. Often, a person fears the reaction of others to his "bad" feelings, and hence buries these feelings, either consciously or subconsciously. This denial results in the self-destructive behaviors that I have listed above.

For example, a child who feels secure about expressing anger towards his parents—who can share his fears in the expectation of being loved and comforted—is unlikely to be a child with terrible nightmares. Conversely, a child who fears his parents' wrath will most likely hide his anger towards them, only to have it return in the form of nightmares, bedwetting, etc.

If we could show our children that negative feelings are a part of living; that negative feelings can be felt and endured; that they gradually go away; that they are not overwhelming or poisonous; that they can and should be acknowledged and shared—then, our children would be better off. Fewer of our teenagers would try to avoid these feelings by drowning them in alcohol or drugs, or even suicide attempts. By these acts, our teenagers are only doing what society has taught them so well—to avoid pain and frustration, to bury it at any cost.

Buried anger is very often turned against the self. A child will think along these lines: "If Mommy and Daddy say that anger is bad and I am angry, then I must be bad. If I am bad, then I deserve to be punished." The child, or child-grown adult, will then contrive different ways to punish himself. One of the saddest phenomena that I have observed in my practice over the years is that of the intelligent, attractive, talented, decent person who has made his own life hell by turning his rage and pain inwards and punishing himself for the sins of his parents.

A lovely and accomplished woman sat in the chair across from me weekly and railed at herself continuously for not being a "perfect person." Her complaints took many forms. She was not married, she had not gone far enough in her career, she was five pounds overweight, she had a pimple or two on her face.

She felt stupid and worthless, unable to make her problems go away. She hammered at herself endlessly in rage, not acknowledging her wonderful qualities, the realistic goals she had achieved, and the positive aspects of her life. She could not conceive of the good life she would enjoy if she had, at a young age, been able to express her anger at her mother for unrealistic expectations, instead of internalizing her mother's perfectionistic desires and turning her rage against herself.

There is controversy today in our society about madness and what its origins are—genetic, chemical, environmental. It is my belief that at least one great cause of madness is unprocessed feelings or rage, pain and helplessness. The catatonic person withdraws from the world in one great, final gulp because the world is too terrible to be experienced. His rage and hatred is such that he must get rid of it. Had he allowed himself to feel and express his primitive rage, it might have dissipated, rather than accrued into a bomb.

Similarly, people like the Son of Sam victimize entire populations, yet are described as having been quiet or pleasant. This type of psychotic has split off his rage for years and hidden it, until it will no longer be imprisoned. Then it springs forth in visions of avenging devils and dogs and orders to kill, myth in the formation of madness.

In his book *Going Crazy*, Otto Friedrich chronicles a woman's journey from sanity to madness and back again. She worked her way out of her madness by hours of primal screaming meant to release her inordinate rage. Hinckley, in his attempt to kill the president, probably tried to discharge in one great cry all the rage he had built up over the years against his father and transferential authority figures. Were his killing rage allowed expression early on; were it acknowledged, understood and tempered by sensitive parenting, the shot might not have been fired.

As Christopher Marlowe says in *Hero and Leander*, "It lies not in our power to hate, for will in us is overruled by fate." Feelings are not willed. We come equipped with a full measure of emotions, just as we come equipped with a full set of 32 teeth. And if we could acknowledge and accept all our feelings, we would be on our way to an emotionally healthier society.

As we are greatly uncomfortable with certain feelings, so we are uncomfortable with our human frailties. There is a call in our society for human "perfection" in persona and relationships. it begins at the moment of birth, when the doctor announces to the mother that she's had a "perfect" baby. Everyone gathers around, cooing, "What a perfect baby!"

Why a "perfect" baby? Why not a healthy baby, or a fine baby, or simply a baby? Already, we are setting up unrealistic expectations. "Perfect" babies do not cry, throw up, wake up their parents, or need constant diaper changing. In other words, "perfect" babies do not exist.

But say this baby thrives, prospers, and grows into a 3 year old. Home comes Daddy from the office, greets her with affection, throws her in the air and asks the momentous question, "Were you a good girl today?"

Daddy, in his playful mood, does not realize the unplayful message that he is transmitting to his daughter. She hears, "Tell me that you did everything 'right' today. Tell me that you made no one angry. Tell me that you didn't have any 'mean' or 'naughty' feelings. Tell me what I want to hear so that I can approve of you today."

What would happen if Daddy were to say simply, "How was your day, honey?" or "Tell me about your day and I'll tell you about mine." What would happen if he then told her about the mistakes he made at work and the fight he had with his boss, or else if he told her how tired he was and how glad he was to see her?

She might learn that life and people consist of strengths and weaknesses, power and frailty, mistakes and solutions, joy and sorrow. She might learn that she could make mistakes or be angry and still be a worthwhile person, rather than the bad monster her daddy's "good girl" question implies.

When my daughter was just 3 years old, we were at a wedding, and the inevitable question was asked her: "Are you a good girl?" She responded, "Sometimes I'm a good girl. Sometimes I'm a bad girl. In general, I'm OK." It was one of those moments when a mother feels she's doing something right.

But I remember other moments, one when she was 4 years old. We were leaving a dance recital where she had performed adequately and happily, but not with great energy and concentration. I berated her for five minutes with a lecture on discipline. I didn't want my daughter to be adequate and content; I wanted her perfect, a genius, a disciplined performer at four. I couldn't glow with the fact that I had a healthy, growing child. I needed her to be perfect and special. Any acceptance of passivity as a personality trait for her was out.

I was repeating the hue and cry of perfection that echoes everywhere, from every rafter. I heard it in my mother's voice when I brought home seven A's and three B's. She wanted to know why I didn't have all A's.

I hear it in the countless television advertisements for plastic surgery. They advise us to fix our noses or chins, as though an imperfect or irregular feature is a deterrent to a good life. Scores of women strain and starve to lose those last ten pounds, so that their figures can conform to the societal mode of perfection displayed in jeans ads.

I hear it in the anguished voice of a teenager who tries to get rid of his last three pimples because only perfect skin can win him a date with a desirable girl. I hear it in the depressed and humiliated voices of the seniors who were not accepted by the "right" college. They feel that going to one of the less reputable colleges shows their parents and everyone at large that they are inadequate—not good enough—doomed to a life of worthlessness and failure. Non-acceptance to a "good" college seems, to them, to confirm their sense of worthlessness as people.

Can I tell them that many people I admire for being kind and decent and living full, honorable lives have never gone to college? They would not believe me, probably, because they have been raised to believe that the college one is accepted to is a measure of personhood, and that a "smart" person gets into a "good". college.

People rage at themselves with shame because they "only" make $20,000 a year, as if salary were a measure of their personhood. Our culture teaches us that the more one earns, the more "successful" and hence "better" one is. I hear it in different voices and different versions every day: "He's so handsome. If only he were smarter." . . . "She's a nice girl, his fiancée, but she never went to college." . . . "My friends don't have to be in love with a man to have sex with him, but I do. What's wrong with me?"

And so it goes . . . on and on. In every individual home and in every aspect of our society, there is a message that one should strive to be perfect, and that our worth and value as people are measured by how close to perfection we come. Few people seem to notice that these messages are crazy and inconsistent; that the standards vary from home to home and society to society. For although the standards vary, they persist; we measure ourselves against them, and many of us find ourselves wanting and worthless.

Years of experience working with children and adults have taught me many things. This is most important: *Love, accept,* and *embrace* your children as they are with all their strengths, frailties, gifts and problems. They will then learn to love and accept themselves as they are, and that self-esteem will serve as the underlying safety net that secures their mental health.

What I have outlined will prove a very difficult task for most of us. It means changing our way of thinking about ourselves and the way we communicate with others. It means analyzing ourselves and thinking about why we have placed this awesome burden of "perfection" on ourselves and others. It means monitoring our actions and responses.

For example, if a young child tosses around a pet gerbil in play, it means not saying, "It's stupid to throw gerbils." It means saying, instead, "It's normal to be curious about creatures and what they can do, but we don't throw gerbils, because it hurts them."

Instead of saying, "Get a better report card and I'll buy you the bike you always wanted," we must learn to say, "You seem to be having problems with certain subjects. What's difficult for you and how can I help?"

A human being is not a perfect creation. He is a wonderfully, exquisitely, elegantly complicated and varied organism of infinite beauty and variety. If we could liberate ourselves and accept ourselves in all our glory and stupidity, majesty and inconsequence; if we could marvel at our paradoxes and laugh with glee at our state, we would be a long way towards our salvation.

I can foresee the complaints and objections at this point. "So, she wants us to accept the criminals and the drug addicts and the alcoholics. See if she can live with a kid who steals, and just let him steal."

But that's not my point. If a child steals, we should help him not to steal. But the best way to do this is not to treat him as just "a stealer." Perhaps he is a carpenter or an artist, perhaps he loves his baby cousin and plays with him . . . we must focus on the positive aspects of his personality, rather than on just the negative ones.

This does not mean that we should negate or disregard his negative behaviors. It merely means that we should love and accept all of him—love the thief while helping him to give up stealing.

Every day, I work on my perfectionistic personality. Every day, I try not to be too demanding of myself and others. Every day, I try to change this trait in myself which is not productive, but I don't hate myself for it. I'm not "bad" because of it. I accept my perfectionism and embrace it as a part of my totality, while still trying to change it to a more healthy and useful form.

Yesterday, I met my neighbor in the lobby. She is a helpful, intelligent, pleasant lady. Our schedules are different, but, occasionally, we talk. She told me about her son—about how well he was doing in college, and about his being the captain of the soccer team. I told her that my daughter liked her classes, but that she was lonely, finding it difficult to find a boyfriend and a new set of friends.

Her eyes blanked. She never responded, but began to talk about something else. She was uncomfortable with the idea that my daughter's life was not perfect. She was probably uncomfortable with the idea that her son's life was not perfect. She never talked about his ulcer or the fact that he had always had few friends.

A year ago, in a television interview, Christina DeLorean spoke at great length about her happy marriage and wonderful family life. A more perfect union could hardly be imagined.

A year later, she is telling a court that her husband pursued a jet set life, was never home, paid no attention to the children. What then was the point of previously painting a false and perfect picture? The point was probably to enhance self-esteem. Thus, to feel OK about oneself and admirable to others is to be perceived as perfect and having a perfect life. How many celebrities talk about the pain of living with a rebellious teenager, the rage of dealing with an unfaithful husband, the helplessness of depression, or the anxiety of waiting for the next job?

They don't. They weave the myth of perfect lives because only that is admired and approved by a misguided public. Even when problems are admitted—like Betty Ford's alcohol addiction or Rock Hudson's and Magic Johnson's bout with AIDS—the people involved are cast as conquering heroes, bravely seeking a positive resolution. The pain, the struggle, the years of hiding and lying are not addressed. Only the "good" can be exposed. All else is shameful.

As Max Lerner tells us in *America as a Civilization*:

> Rarely is there support for the brooding
> exploration of the whole enriching range
> of emotional life in a culture as rich
> and complex as the American. [pp. 577-8]

The myths hold. We learn that if we have problems—in our lives, careers, marriages or families—we are bad or unsuccessful. We feel embarrassed and ashamed, instead of understanding that problems and disappointments are a normal and inevitable part of every life.

If we could only accept that truth, we could open ourselves to each other. We could share our travails and solutions and be there to support each other. We would be better prepared for difficulty. We would understand that therapy is not an admission of failure and defeat but simply a way of learning to accept and cope well with the problems of living.

The tale goes that once upon a time, Moses complained to God about the children of Israel. He felt that they were stiff-necked and contentious. Thereupon God chastised Moses, saying, "I have not created them angels, but flesh and blood, fallible human beings. Therefore, do not expect them to act as angels. Since they are mortal, it is natural that they should have the limitations and imperfections of flesh and blood, mortal human beings."

If God can accept and love us in our imperfections, why can we not accept and love ourselves?

LOVE MYTHS

Every Valentine's Day, a chubby little fellow appears, hauling his arrows and ready to strike at the hearts of lovers. By now, we know that Cupid is a myth, and that falling in love is not due to being pierced by a falling arrow. However, countless other myths about love still abound. Blithely and masochistically, we hold them to our hearts.

Primary is the myth of loving. I once heard Ashley Montagu, the anthropologist, make one of the wisest statements I have ever heard on love and loving. He said, "Everyone talks about love, and only 2% of the population can do it."

That has also been my experience. Everywhere one turns, love is being given lip service. "I love him desperately." . . . "He's my child, of course I love him." . . . "I love my country." . . . "She loves him but she can't live with him." . . . "How can you do this to someone you love?" . . . "I love my job." . . . "I love those cupcakes."

We have lost, if we ever understood, the meaning of the word. Webster's Dictionary devotes an entire paragraph to defining love:

(1A)   a feeling of strong personal attachment induced by that which delights or commands admiration, by sympathetic understanding or by ties of kinship.

(1B)   the principle or quality of which this feeling is a manifestation; also, a personification.

(2)   the benevolence attributed to God as being like a father's affection for his children; also, man's adoration for God in attitude or devotion.

(3)   strong liking; fondness, goodwill, usually applied to persons as in greetings to objects of ideal regard as . . . love of learning, love of freedom.

(4)   tender and passionate affection for one of the opposite sex, as to marry without love.

(5)   the object of affection; sweetheart; often employed in endearing address.

(6)   sexual passion.

(7)   Cupid, Eros as God of love, Venus.

(8)   a thin silk stuff, a border made of it.

(9)   (9A) the virgin's bower of Europe.

(10)   (9B) a love plant.

(11)   a dear, a darling, as in "Isn't he a love?"

(12)   Christian Science: A synonym for God.

(13)   Tennis: no points scored.

It seems clear that the Webster writers are confused and struggling to integrate into the definition all the popular uses of the word. I submit to you that what we name as "love" is often something quite else. It may be infatuation, sexual passion, dependent attachment, need, liking, admiration, duty, intellectual interest, need to merge. All these needs and feelings are often garbed and masked in the cloak of love.

I feel that the true definition of love is a feeling of deep affection and tenderness and caring for the other, such that one is as concerned for the other's well-being as one is for one's own. One who truly loves acts to express that tenderness and concern with acts of support, empathy, nurturance and warmth. Thus, for me, love is not only a feeling, but it is active—it acts to express itself appropriately.

In romantic love, sexual passion is a component of the whole. As Dr. Gadpaille delineates in *Cycles of Sex*:

> Adult sexual love is the capacity to
> invest both sexual and tender feelings in
> the same person and to hold that person's
> well-being as important as one's own.
> [p. 317]

2

In *A Dialogue with Erik Erikson*, Erikson describes intimacy as arriving out of a successful completion of the stage of young adulthood. He describes it as "the real ability to fuse your identity with somebody else without the fear that you're going to lose something yourself." Out of this stage emerges "the ability to care—to care for somebody, to care to do something for somebody, to take care of the other when they need protection."

The ability to love is a quality that needs to be nurtured and developed through man's long childhood. A person's growing up will need to be so successful that he or she emerges from it with the capacity to trust, to hope, to have purpose, to work, to be faithful and to care. The capacity to love is not a given. It is a hard-won achievement for a person who has successfully transversed the oral stage of self-love, self-preoccupation; the anal stage of power struggle and ambivalence; the phallic stage of exhibitionism; transversed the oedipal complex; on through the adolescent struggle for separation, search for identity; and through the young adult stage of searching for autonomy and intimacy. It presupposes that one has had parents who themselves had the capacity to love and that one's holding environment and experiences and world have been "good enough" to allow for a happy conclusion of the growing tasks of man's long childhood—the greatest of which is the capacity to love.

We do unspeakable things in the name of love. For the love of our country, we slaughter and mutilate thousands of human beings whose only crime is that their interests are different from ours. For the love of God, we kill as many in so-called religious wars. For the love of a wife, we beat her regularly; for the love of a husband, we nag and berate him until there remains no vestige of self-esteem left for him. For the love of our children, we scold and correct and try to mold them into our own self-image, until they have no identity or authenticity or selfhood that remains.

And so it goes. "The fault, dear Brutus, is not in our stars, but in ourselves." The fault, dear readers, lies not in love but in ourselves—in our capacity for it and understanding of it. Were we to be honest about what love means, we could search ourselves to see if we possessed it. It is an unfortunate paradox of American life that while the American man or woman may be obsessed with romantic love because it is the only socially acceptable secular escape from the individualistic prison of the self, he or she is not good at the real art of loving. This is an acquisitive society fueled by money, power and success. In such a society, love is charged with the power and violence of the acquisitive drive. The young American cultivates love, not as a tender, cooperative, empathic, creative relationship between like-minded people, but as a testing ground of virility. Courtship becomes a matter of personal success in a quest where the goal is that of proving himself. In marriage, the person who is a hard-headed, competitive operator finds it hard to change his mode when he comes home at night. The sense of loneliness, the hunger for fulfillment, the search for identity becomes tangled with the compulsion to power while love waits outside. To reverse that would require a light shaft, laser-beam penetration of honesty as to our true condition.

We would not offer marriage if we could not promise intimacy. We would not have children if we could not offer selflessness. We could get the help we need in developing the capacity to love. We could develop systems of parenting, raising and educating children so as to help them manage the various stages of childhood successfully, emerging as loving adults.

I sigh as I write this and stop to question myself as to what the sigh is about. A sadness envelops me and a hopelessness that a narcissistic society that has enthroned self-gratification can hear a plea for movement away from that which to the narcissistic person seems crucial and life-sustaining and absolutely fundamental.

I remember President Carter and how we totally dismissed him when he attempted to address the issue of our narcissistic society and its ailments. I remember the book *Our Narcissistic Culture*, and how little attention and discussion it received. It is hard to get a baby, entranced with its own navel, to stop and look onward. Yet we must try, in the interest of our own survival.

LOVE MYTHS – 2

The lights go up. Strains of romantic music reverberate in the room. A beautiful blonde girl glides into the room, beaming. On the sidelines, an all-American boy jostles his friend's arm. "I don't know who she is but that's the girl I'm going to marry!" End of scene. Love at first sight! How often have we read these stories in magazines, seen them on television or been enthralled by them in movies. Tipper Gore tells us that her meeting with Al was "almost" love at first sight. How much is this idea—love at first sight—part of our society's mythology—and how absurd! How can one love someone about whom one knows nothing? Perhaps we can say that there is lust at first sight or chemical attraction or the vision of someone who fits our idealized version of our mate, or perhaps we are so ready to fall in love that the object is not of too much consequence, but. . . love at first sight is an impossibility. To care for a stranger as we do for ourselves is an attribute possessed mainly by saints. For another human being to be able to be real to us, we must know him, his history, his character, his preferences, his hopes, his dreams. We must have time to experience him, to interact with him, to spend time with him in many diverse and varied situations, before we can be clear about who he is, who we are with him and what the feelings are.

I know an intelligent woman who regularly discards men after a first date: "I didn't feel anything for him. I wasn't comfortable with him. We have nothing in common." are the excuses she generally gives. She has bought the idea of love at first sight. In her case love means an instant sexual attraction and an inappropriate sense of intimacy—feeling very close to someone who is a virtual stranger. Inevitably, the relationships she forms peter out quickly and are sometimes painful, always disappointing. These men, who are sexually attractive and instantly warm and accessible, also turn out to be liars, deceivers, immature, incapable of true intimacy, etc.—not objects of true love.

What this attractive young woman doesn't realize is that relationships take time. It is normal to feel uncomfortable, anxious and awkward with a stranger. It is normal, at the beginning of a relationship, not to see the common ground. Even sexual attraction can sneak up on you gently and quietly in a very satisfactory way. It doesn't have to hit you over the head. We must learn to tiptoe gingerly into a relationship with our eyes wide open, to give it much time and patience, to nurture it and work at it and see what emerges. Sometimes, like a rose, love will slowly bloom and grow; sometimes it will be friendship and sometimes an understanding that this relationship cannot or should not be sustained and, then, we continue each in our separate direction.

Last night, I saw a 25 year old girl who was coming for help only 5 months after her marriage. She was being plagued by severe headaches and backaches that she had previously never experienced. Slowly and painfully she began to talk of her frustrations and confusion about this relationship. Her husband swore he loved her and cared for her. Yet although she, too, had a very demanding full-time job, he refused to do a particle of housework. "It all belongs to her," he exclaimed. "Only men who are wimps do housework." He would not allow her to buy a washing machine out of the wedding gift money and insisted that she cart the dirty laundry from their apartment in the Bronx to his mother's house in Queens to wash it. Although she was supporting him through medical school, he would become enraged if she so much as spent $50.00 on a pair of shoes that she needed. When, abused by a nasty mother-in-law, she turned to her husband for help, he walked away, claiming it was not his issue.

At this point, Charlotte was crying bitterly and berating herself for not having seen her husband as he really was. "Being in love," she had failed to adequately notice the permeating rage and physical abusiveness in her husband's home, her husband's totally passive stance when she needed his help in various situations, his cheapness, etc. Charlotte had fallen both for the love at first sight myth—they had met at a dance and "knew instantly" that they were for each other—and the "we love each other" myth which makes marriage inevitable. She had not stopped to look critically and realistically at her romance, to unwind the strands of love and see, beneath, the reality of what was happening. She had not taken the time to understand her husband's personality, the dynamics and patterns of their duet and the consequences of these patterns on their future life together. And here she was five months hence, ill, anxious and stressed, with a husband who refused to come for help and to admit that there was anything wrong with the marriage. There are many Bobs and Charlottes and Teds and Alices amongst us who set sail into marriage with the paddle of "love at first sight" as a guide. It is not a compass to steer a marriage by.

Her blue hair sparkled, her black mesh stockings gleamed and her jewelry jangled. "I met this really cool boy," she revealed. "I'm in love." She didn't know him. He had stood in front of her at the rock concert. He had flowing black hair to his waist, earrings in his nose, black leather outfit and very blue eyes and it was . . . "love at first sight." Inwardly, I groaned. The generations change but the harming myths remain.

The girl is 18 years old. She is blonde, beautiful, intelligent, charming and very lovable. She doesn't have a boyfriend. She doesn't understand. "Why don't I have a boyfriend?" she keeps repeating. "What's wrong with me?" The implication, one that I've heard so many times before, is that she's not lovable. If she were, someone would be in love with her. Sometimes, the same idea appears in a different guise. A person is rejected by a love object and, again, immediately the assumption is that the rejection is an indication of one's own non-lovability. Nonsense. One can be very lovable and not have a mate. Perhaps one is not or does not place oneself in a position to meet romantic possibilities. Perhaps one has appropriately high expectations for the love object. It will then take lots of time and energy to find the right person. Perhaps one appears so "special" that others fear to be rejected and will not approach. Perhaps a man will reject a lady (or vice versa) because she is too intelligent or too attractive and he feels more comfortable with a dumber or plainer mate. Perhaps you will be rejected because your love object is masochistic and unconsciously wants someone who will hurt him rather than someone like you who will give him tender loving care. Perhaps she wants a Jewish man like Daddy and will reject you because you aren't or will reject you because she doesn't want a Jewish man like Daddy and you are. Perhaps someone won't love you because they like to play chasing games and you, who doesn't play games, approach too closely and, thus, can't be chased. The variations and computations of people's choices and non-choices are endless. The salient point to be made is brief. Because you are, at this moment, not loved, not chosen, or rejected, that does not make you a non-lovable person. I know hundreds of destructive, hostile, malicious people who are married, have big families and wide circles of friends, and others who are decent and caring and lovable who are alone or, at

Miriam Kove

least, less well endowed. This is not a fair or just world and we must not look for logic. We must also not allow our worth or lovability to be adjudicated by others from the outside. Every one of us has lovable qualities. We must nurture them and appreciate them, increase them, and love ourselves, respect ourselves, esteem ourselves, and—if we are open, and reach out and have patience—in time, there will be others who will love us.

"LIVING HAPPILY EVER AFTER" MYTH

Eva Bronson is 43 years old. She has two grown children, a daughter who is a reporter and one who is trying to establish herself as a singer. She is attractive and intelligent and hard-working. She has, however, no education past high school and now that she has divorce papers in her hands, she has few marketable skills and very little chance of making it in the marketplace. How did this happen to Eva, who was an A student all through high school and class president and homecoming queen? It happened because when Eva was 13, she fell in love with Larry, and from then on there was no other man for her. When they married at 18, Eva was sure that they were going to "live happily ever after" in the style of the '50s. Larry was going to bring home the bacon and she was going to be wife and mother. When Larry brought home the babysitter and informed Eva that they were in love and he was leaving Eva, Eva was forced to realize that she wasn't going to "live happily ever after."

Marilyn Nichols met Marc Andrews when she was 23 and she fell in love. They courted for a year and a half, and Marc vacillated between charming love and attention and withdrawal and coldness. Unable to commit himself to this or any other relationship fully, he nevertheless informed her that he was ready to marry. Marilyn breathed a sigh of relief. Now that they were to be married, all the coldness and distancing and ambivalence would cease, because, after all, once people married, people "lived happily ever after." Marilyn was not stupid nor was she severely disturbed. She was extremely naïve and had bought the "happily ever after" myth in its entirety. Today, 20 years later, she is seriously contemplating divorce. Alas, she had not lived happily ever after. The coldness, the distancing, the selfishness, the ambivalence had continued into all the years of the marriage and had caused much anguish and pain.

George Silow met and married his second wife after a painful divorce. Although his first marriage had been horribly disillusioning in so many ways, he knew that this one would be different. In this one, he would live happily ever after. Well, this one was different. There was love and warmth, companionship and understanding. They divided tasks; they supported; they nurtured; they were happy.

9

Unfortunately, however, George Silow did not live happily ever after. Five years after he married her, Estelle died of a sudden heart attack.

There is, often, no "happily ever after." With hope, with goodwill, with prayer, we enter a relationship. But we don't know its course and we don't know its outcome, and it's the humility of that knowledge that can save us from false expectations, false beliefs and promises, that can aid to prepare us for the surprises of the future, to look at each day as it is, to enjoy what we have and to work at what is wrong and not to live in the stupor, the falseness, the ambivalence and denial of "happily ever after."

In 1950 the well-known psychoanalyst Bruno Bettelheim published a book, *Love is Not Enough*, in which the main tenet was that growing children rely not only on love, but upon adult care that feeds both spoken and unspoken needs. In other words, it's not enough to feel affection, concern for your child. One must *act*, and act in the child's best interest. To know what the interests are, we must know about child development. For instance, when a child first starts walking, he is aglow with great expectations and consumed with curiosity about this new, accessible wonderful world. If he is touching everything and breaking everything and being scolded and told "no" too often, he may decide that this wonderful world is not wonderful but dangerous and that exploration and curiosity are taboo. A knowledgeable parent can "make the house safe" for a toddler by putting away the doodads, glass tables, sharp-edged statues, and let him roam and discover. How many parents know to do that? When children are very young, they believe they cause things to happen and feel bad and ashamed and guilty when "bad" things happen around them. How many parents know that and know how to help children understand that "bad happenings" are not their fault? In adolescence, it is normal to go through a phase where there is sexual experimentation with the same sex. How many parents would act sane and accepting and explain the phenomenon to their adolescent if they were to "catch" him or her in this experience or hear about it? How many of us understand the different stages of childhood and that appropriate discipline is different for different stages? How many of us understand where excessive permissiveness is as threatening and anxiety-producing for the child as harsh discipline? Every day, on talk shows, I see millions of parents stand up and assert a loving home as the criterion for well-being and I think—how we perpetuate this

10

myth—how "mad" we are becoming on this false belief system. No, Virginia, "Love is not enough"—not in parenting, not in relationships, not at all. A sister is being yelled at by another sister. "You've been away to college and you haven't written for six months." The answer comes, "But you know I love you." Love is not enough. The second sister has hurt the first by ignoring her need for attention, compassion and sharing. A husband sits next to his wife at a table of friends. "She's going to make sissies of my kids," he sneers, "always coddling them and telling them to turn the other cheek. I love her but I don't know." Love is not enough. He is not addressing her need to be respected and her view to be respected and her need not to be shamed and abused in front of her peers. A member of a fundamentalist Christian group arises. "I love everyone in this room," he says, "but only those who know Jesus will enter the Kingdom of Heaven." If he loves me so much, why doesn't he respect my need and my right for a different belief system? And so it goes. No . . . love is not enough. It needs to be accompanied by knowledge, understanding and attention and respect for the spoken and unspoken needs of those we say we love.

As years march onward, new myths are added to old ones in this lexicon of madness. In the '60s and '70s, there was the onslaught of the "multiple orgasm." Suddenly, it had been discovered that we had been doing sex wrong all these years, that one orgasm was definitely not enough, and that human beings were capable of and entitled to numerous orgasms. Articles appeared everywhere on this new phenomenon, what it was, what it felt like and how to get it. I remember the intelligent, educated woman in my consciousness raising group talking at length and with great pain about the new discovery. They had only one orgasm at a time, what was wrong with them? Was there something wrong with their husbands? Various techniques were discussed and exchanged and every week, there were reports on progress or lack of it. These were not wealthy, indolent women. These were hard-working, struggling young mothers who had busy, complicated lives but who once again had been caught in the trap of "you're not doing it right." They hardly stopped to ask themselves if they were happy with their sex life, satisfied, felt loved, warmth . . . They were chasing yet another myth, perpetuated on them by the media, by a sexologist looking for a buck, by sex shop operator, by who knows who.

With the multiple orgasm theory came the "how many times a week do you do it?" theory. Again, the emphasis is not on personal rhythms, desires, wants, satisfactions related only to the couple concerned; the emphasis is on a scale of "achievement" where five times a week is better than two times a week, etc. . . and people are struggling to maintain a national average rather than personal pleasure. How silly to be concerned with the Joneses when the issue is so individual, personal and private.

That was the 60s and 70s. In the 80s and 90s we had the myth of the "Divorce Romance." By now, 50% of us in this country have discovered that we are not going to live happily ever after, at least in this marriage, and we are getting ready for divorce. With what are we to replace the fantasy of Cinderella and her prince, love at first sight and happily ever after? A fantasy needs to be replaced by another fantasy—enter the Divorce Romance. This is the dream where the 45 year old divorced woman steps sadly into the world, immediately obtains an executive management job which nets her $75,000 a year and the praise and admiration of her superiors, finds herself surrounded by interesting, attractive men who take her to lunch, dinner, theatre, the opera and, romantically and passionately to bed. Meanwhile, her children have grown miraculously independent, assumed household chores, understood the value of their mother's work, emulate her as a role model and view her as superwoman. In a year or two, the right man will come along for marriage and she will, then, truly have everything.

The man's fantasy is different. After divorce, he will move into a beautiful condo with a pool. His main furniture will be a bar with every drink known to man. There will be a few easy, comfortable pieces of furniture—no draperies, knickknacks and plants to water. A woman will come to clean and launder and shop and attend to those dreary household chores he wants to know nothing about. He will work at his job all the hours that he wants without having to report to anyone his comings or goings. On off days, he will fish, golf and bed a variety of nubile, gorgeous, sexy young blondes who will find him irresistible and fuck his socks off. When he finds time, he will take his kids to the zoo. They will be thrilled to see him and they'll all have a wonderful time together.

Let's stop dreaming for a moment. The average woman who divorces either has not been trained for a career or has been out of the market for a considerable time. It will be difficult for her to manage employment. Tom Andrews, an executive search firm executive, describes the market for returning women into the work force as "bleak." "If they have few marketable skills," he says, ". . . and need to earn a salary that will help them support a family, they will probably have to go into commission-related business such as selling real estate. The catch 22 is that in these occupations, the given salary is minimal and building up commissions is slow, so that one has to look forward to pressure, stress, years of very low money-making, working round the clock. For women who have professions, the picture is more attractive. Yet they, too, are in a difficult position. No matter their age, life experience, etc., they will be hired to start at the bottom, at trainee or advanced trainee situations. There will be little money or status for them and less opportunity since they are considered by companies less desirable than recent college graduates since college kids are considered as having more developmental potential."

Prime Minister Shimon Peres, when addressing a conference of Zionist women, quoted for them an astonishing statistic. He said that of the entire world work force, ½ is women, that they do 2/3 of the work and receive 1/10 of the pay. Though, of course, the situation is different in various countries and hopefully much better in our country than in others, still the graph remains consistent here too. What women can look forward to is more work, less pay, and very little status.

My friends in the business community tell me that it's still very much a "man's world out there." Women who are smart and aggressive may be useful but they're not liked, not appreciated. "Father knows best" has not yet left the boardrooms. If you know how to do something better or in a way that will be more effective or more productive for the company or you have a smarter idea than the boss has, you had better learn to couch it in the mildest, most tentative, most deprecating of styles. There must be no hint of negativity. Then, of course, there is sexual harassment. There would be no need for sexual harassment laws were there not enough evidence of sexual harassment in the workplace. In the job, as at home, we need to be the self-effacing, compliant workhorse or the sexual object or the adoring worshipper. Women, everywhere, are striving to make themselves

13

heard as whole, competent, assertive people but the world has not yet adjusted to their voice.

So having survived a long and tiring and stress-filled day at the office, the woman is returning home to cook the dinner, make the beds, pay the bills and wash the clothes, fix the sink, supervise the homework, worry about the strange sounds in the car. Meanwhile, the kids have not miraculously turned into miniature adults. They are children. They need attention, supervision, advice. They need someone to listen to their problems when they're ready to share, to make sure they follow the limits that need to be followed, to give them the sense of comfort and security and protection. It is inappropriate for children to have to be burdened by fears about money, to have to mother their mother, cleaning the house when they should be playing with their friends. What I am saying is that not only do kids not miraculously turn into adults, but that we shouldn't want them to and help them not to, that a good mother needs to struggle to help a child remain a child and give him the nurturing, time, love, attention he deserves—an enormously difficult task for an already burdened soul. And then . . . since children (hopefully) will be children, there is the fighting of siblings, the screeching of the stereo, the endless ring of the telephone, the harsh accusations and the sullen silence and since there is only you, it's all on you . . .

But wait . . . that gorgeous guy will come in in a minute and make it all better . . . take you away from all this to champagne and a view of the river. Hold it a moment. What gorgeous guy are we speaking of? Most of the eligible men in your age group are married or taken. Many of those who are not are gay or chasing little twenty-two year olds in Central Park or along the Club Med beaches. Then, there is a small percentage of divorced men, so bruised and battered that they need full-time care or so pathological that no self-loving woman would want to go near them or so broke from alimony and child support that they can't afford to buy you dinner. You're not pessimistic, however; you know that, out there, there must be some decent guys who want to love and be loved. Where will you meet them? At the bars, on the subways, in the supermarket? Well . . . what about Mr. Goodbar? What about the fact that payment for a drink is often going to bed with a stranger?

Are the divorced men having more fun? Are they really bedding sexy young ladies day and night? Well . . . some of them are . . . but it takes a lot of energy to keep up with girls in their 20s. Most 50 year old men don't have it and worry about heart attacks. It's difficult to find community, empathy and understanding with someone who has twenty years less experience of life than you do. Yes, Joe, there is a generation gap. Young women want babies and families. Many middle-aged men have families and don't want the work and burden and obligations of new ones. And then there is the difficulty of approaching women. For someone out of the dating game for 20-30 years, it's not easy to learn the routine once again, a changed game, a difficult game, ending with the possibility of the same old rejection. And, at home, there is no one to clean, no one to cook, no one to listen, no one to comfort. Most men cannot afford maids and suddenly they're the ones who have to clean the stove and buy the groceries and worry about the shirts and most of them are clumsy at it and resentful and deprived. Cooking an omelette in a dirty, lonely apartment is not all it's cracked up to be. Well . . . you'll see the kids on Sunday, but they are not as happy to see you as you thought. You're keeping them from a picnic or party they wanted to attend, and anyway, they're mad that you're not living at home anymore and you're not sure what to say to them because a whole week in their lives of momentous events has passed and you weren't there. You don't know that they chipped their tooth, that the washing machine broke and they fixed it, that their teacher accused them of cheating and Mommy fixed it. Suddenly, you're a stranger and the conversation is polite and stilted and hostile and everyone is eating too much and trying too hard to have fun and you're running out of places to take them or ways of entertaining them. And you drop them off and go home and think about what a failure you are and how you're really too old to start over again or you bury yourself in your work and deny the emptiness and loneliness or you run after women to deny the emptiness and loneliness or you attach yourself quickly to someone you don't really want and are not really ready for to deny the emptiness and loneliness. Statistics show that single men are the most unhappy and they die at the youngest age.

Am I proposing, then, that we forget about divorce? No . . . when a marriage is not working, when there is rage and hate and lack of support and understanding between the partners, when a relationship is causing people more grief and pain than joy, when it is not allowing partners to bloom and grow . . . the relationship needs to be dissolved.

What I am proposing is that we look at divorce and its aftermath, not at its myth, but realistically, so that knowing the facts we can address them and make the situation easier and less painful for ourselves.

1) The first important consideration is not to act on our feelings. We might hate our mate and want to demolish him with words or deeds. We might want revenge and think of taking out an ad in *The New York Times* to tell everyone what a bastard he is or we might feel totally helpless about our fate and just let things happen. I suggest that though we're probably feeling very intensely, we go beyond these feelings and try to deal with the reality of the situation.

2) Ask yourself some important questions. Is this an amicable divorce? Are both parties agreed that this is the road to go? If so, then it would be a good idea to opt for *divorce mediation*. In divorce mediation, a person who is knowledgeable in law, psychology, child custody, family issues discusses the problems with the divorcing couple, helps them to negotiate a fair settlement, teaches them how to handle the situation with the children. Generally, the couple goes for approximately 10 sessions. It removes the need for lawyers, removes the adversary positions, is much less expensive financially and makes for much better feeling and mental health for the entire family.

3) Often, the divorce is not amicable. The wife has decided to leave. The husband doesn't want her to and would be enraged if he were to know. Here is where reality enters. If the wife is established in a career and feels capable of managing life on her own, is certain that she can get custody of the children and a reasonable settlement, she may decide to file for divorce immediately. However, often it is not the best of all possible worlds. There are many situations where the wife is not ready to be in the marketplace and would, indeed, have a hard time making it. My answer is *prepare*. Every important and difficult transition-moving, marriage, entering college—is better negotiated if prepared for. Several years ago, a friend of mine told her therapist that she was preparing for a divorce and that she would be ready to leave her husband

in three years. The therapist became indignant. "That is no way of divorce," she exhorted. "If you want to leave, leave now." However, she was wrong. That was indeed the way to leave. My friend used her three years to get a masters in education and a city teaching license so that when her divorce came through, she was established in a position where there was enough money and benefits to appropriately raise her family. Her husband, who was a lawyer, had negotiated a settlement for her, where they judge awarded her and her children $8,000.00 a year out of a $100,000.00 annual income. Another friend decided to stay in her marriage for four more years. She used those four years to establish a practice that would provide her a reasonable income and to see her daughter through high school. At that point, her daughter was 18½ years old, past the traumatic teenage years, more able to handle the idea of divorce, and custody was no longer a primary issue. My friend knew that her husband was a self-centered, angry, impulsive man who would sue for custody even though he had been an absent, non-involved parent. According to recent statistics, 70% of men suing for custody are awarded custody, even though many of these men are not the better parent. My friend wanted to manage this traumatic event for herself and her daughter in the most productive way possible and so, she did.

A colleague did not decide to prepare. Enraged by her husband's behavior, she "threw him out." She was left with two children, a boy of four, the other a boy of six months. At that point in time, she was prepared for no career. Her husband promptly took off for Switzerland, where he was unaccountable, while my friend went on welfare and struggled desperately for the next five years until she was able to manage a viable job.

Carolyn Mannes found out that her husband was having an affair. The next afternoon, she packed her bags and with her two young children took a plane to her parents' house in Florida. Hurt and disappointed, she refused to answer his calls and tried to think. A month later, when she was able to speak to him, she discovered that he had sold the house, bought himself a studio apartment and was suing for divorce. Carolyn had nothing to return to. Impulsive action does not help. Thinking, planning and preparing is important, as is reaching out to friendships and to a support system that will be there when the aloneness becomes fact.

4) In this case, the husband has decided to leave. Does he need to prepare? Yes. He needs to think very carefully about the financial situation and how he will manage two households. He needs to explore type and cost of living possibilities. He needs to think about who will manage his household chores and how. Perhaps he can start paying attention to laundry and cooking and household management, that before was left to the partner. He needs to think very carefully about custody and what would be the best situation for the children and how he could manage them and love them if he had them and if not, how would he manage visitation in a way that would allow him to remain a real and living part of his children's lives.

I hasten to add at this moment that I am in no way suggesting a personal and hidden agenda that excludes your partner and focuses only on your future and your needs. To be unhappy in silence, to prepare and plan alone and then, when ready, to take the steps into another life, severing the ties of a committed relationship, is a selfish and ugly betrayal of marriage vows and a total disregard for human decency. Of course, when people are unhappy or frustrated or feel trapped in a relationship, they need to share that with their partner. Both people need to explore together their aims, their situation, their feelings and solutions. Perhaps they can work this through themselves; perhaps they can go to a marriage counselor; perhaps they can see a member of the clergy; join a marriage encounter group; take some time off from each other for solitude and contemplation; even separate domiciles, temporarily, to gain distance and space and try to work through these issues. There are numerous and various options for the caring and concerned and decent couple who want to honor their marriage vows and be fair to themselves, to each other and to their families. Too often, today, the impulsive, greedy, murdering, infantile 18 month old in us wins out and a partner grabs the nearest love object, sees his or her salvation and abandons a spouse and a family, leaving destruction and hate and rage and waste in the wake for everyone concerned.

No—that is a possibility only for the murderous and the sick. Decent people look at themselves, at each other, at their marriage, at reality and try diligently and patiently to solve problems. However, I'm suggesting that if, at the end of that route, the relationships cannot be salvaged, people can then take the time to prepare to separate, doing the co-work that they need to do for themselves and their families, preparing the children, settling the finances, garnishing the individuals skills that they will need to "make" it alone in this world.

That this will be very difficult for people to do when they are scared and enraged and helpless and vicious and vindictive and impulsive, I acknowledge. But do it they must, harboring their own resources, their reality testing, their sense of judgment and fair play, gathering their resources of friends and family and outside professionals to finish unfinished business in a humane way rather than as an exercise of emotion, financial, sometimes physical slaughter.

Too often in our society, the following is the prevailing scenario. A husband in his mid-life crisis feels old, miserable, disenchanted, enraged, unhappy, disappointed in himself and his life. Not understanding that he is in an age-appropriate difficult stage and that these feelings stem from this stage and the unfinished business of his childhood, he displaces these feelings on his spouse. Conflicted and uncertain and made infantile by the regressive nature of the stage, he looks for someone who will instantly "make it all better" and grabs at the nearest available love object, who is usually-and unknowingly to him—a reincarnation of his abusive, neglectful, seductive mother. Suddenly feeling safe and giddy and special with the acquisition of this new partner, he abandons his old family, severing these ties as if they were those of casual acquaintanceship. What usually follows is devastation of the wife, who becomes alcoholic, depressed, suicidal, anorectic or murderous like Jean Harris; confusion and terrible pain and trauma for the children, which is experienced as ulcers, headaches, failure in school, self-destructive behavior or massive denial which now and then erupts in hysterical symptoms. The husband, witnessing this, becomes more enraged as a mechanism to deny his shame and guilt, and starts to punish by withholding money, circulating lies about the spouse or manipulating the children. This will end many years down the road with wounded, traumatized victims. The husband (or wife) who has begun this cycle will end further down the road no better, empty, unhappy, guilty and depressed since he (she) has not addressed the real problems of his psyche and emotional life. Heavily disappointed in the new love object whom he had misidentified, he will drown himself in activity and consumption, pretending to himself and others that he's happy and did "the right thing."

This drama replays itself in our society in a variety of shapes and guises daily. We know it, and, unfortunately, we accept it as a "myth" of what needs to be. I'm suggesting that this "marriage play" is grossly unhealthy and devastating to the individuals and to society and that we must find a better way.

5) What if it looks like you have no choice? What if your spouse comes home one day, announces that he or she is leaving and has begun divorce proceedings? You will probably be shocked, enraged, hysterical, feel powerless, helpless, etc. In the midst of all this terrible pain, there are some ways in which you need to help yourself. Try to find a good lawyer, one who is competent, intelligent, cooperative and responsive. Try to obtain referrals from people whose judgment you trust and respect and who have had actual practical experience with the people to whom you are being recommended. Interview them to find someone with whom you will have a rapport. A husband or wife who leaves the marriage suddenly, with no notice and no mutuality, is someone self-centered and impulsive and not to be trusted. They can and do do anything, including cutting off funds and charge cards, removing furniture, etc. You need an advocate, someone in your corner who will help you protect yourself from this destruction which has been foisted on you. When you have a good lawyer, get yourself a good therapist. Or— get yourself a good therapist and then get yourself a good lawyer.

This is the breakup of a life, and to grieve and understand and put back the pieces is hard, trying and agonizing work, and you need a helping hand and a helping head. Get yourself a support group. Many YMHAs, YMCAs, churches, clinics are running support groups for separated people. People in your situation will understand and know. They are experiencing the same thing. You will feel empathy and nurturance when you most need it, and sharing practical advice can solve problems. Reach out to friends and family and let them in. You will need not to feel so alone and abandoned. Above all, try to be loving and kind to yourself by allowing yourself to experience your feelings and to do what you need to do to cope. Some people become so depressed that every movement is a Herculean task. Some people need to run from place to place and activity to activity to run away from the pain and heartache.

Too many people want to deny everything and have it all better in several weeks, want to "go on with their lives" and beat themselves up emotionally when that's not possible. They are, then, not only experiencing the trauma of the breakup, but also layering that with the shame and guilt of their inadequacy to make in it all OK. When animals are hurt, they wander away and look for a haven in which to lick their wounds. We need to allow ourselves as much. In time, we will work our way through the onslaught and move on-hopefully resurrected, though battered—but we must give ourselves time and patience to journey the process, and the time is different for each of us.

Hand in hand with the desperate need to put it all behind us comes the rage at ourselves, the self-hatred. I'm a failure . . . I made this happen . . . I did everything wrong . . . It's all my fault . . . an endless litany of mea culpas. It's *not* all your fault. Certainly you've made mistakes—but then, you're human, like the rest of us, and problems and frailties are parts of us all. Relationships are very difficult, fraught with danger, and transversing the obstacles is ominous. Both people have to want to do the work and have to be lucky. If your spouse left you this unceremoniously, the "fault" is much more likely to be his. People of care, maturity and mutuality don't leave in this fashion.

Try to be a loving parent to yourself and to live and comfort yourself as you struggle to feel, to know, to understand, to survive and to build.

PARENTING MYTHS

A theory held to the heart in our society, and one closely related to the idea that everyone can love, is that everyone can be a good parent. Morning after morning, people stand up on talk shows, vehement and angry and certain, giving opinions and espousing their capacity to be good parents and their rules for good parenting and, night after night, we hear on the news about the one million runaways, the 4000 yearly teenage suicides, the 28% of the nations tenth and twelfth graders who are addicted to alcohol and the more than one million teenage pregnancies.

Day after day, we hear parents in school auditoriums and principals' offices and neighbors' kitchens making wide generalizations and loud announcements about what their children need, should have, should do and should not do, and every night in the evening newspaper, we read about 11.8% high school dropouts and 300,000 to 600,000 teenage prostitutes and more clinics needing to be opened for teenage psychotics. Why this dichotomy? Why this huge difference between rhetoric and the result? The answer is because we don't, many of us, know how to be good parents and we aren't, and we don't want to face that or face the parenting myths that are leading us astray.

In order to be the professional I am today, in order to know my work, I studied for 16 years of general knowledge and 9 years of particular knowledge relating to my specific discipline. I wrote innumerable papers, was tested hundreds of times, supervised, examined, steered, advised, berated, helped and showed. I read countless books and digested wide varieties of information. Even now, after practicing for 25 years, I consult colleagues when I am in doubt or confused or overinvolved, etc. A secretary would not be hired for her looks and charm and intelligence alone. She has to go to school to study word processing, administration. . . A beautician goes to "beauty school" to learn the arts of shampooing, make-up, permanents, etc. I can think of no occupation or profession where there are not involved special skills, special requirements, and special education and training to develop those occupational skills. Yet, somehow, we assume that men and women can handle the most difficult and responsible and complex and important occupation of all, that of rearing a human being, simply by virtue of their being humans. God gave many of us the ability to procreate. He did not give us the talent, the skill, the knowledge, the patience, the capacity to be good parents. Those we need to acquire for ourselves as we acquire the requisites for being doctors or lawyers or priests or teachers. How do we acquire them? Firstly—by education. Children go through very specific ages or stages in which they have precise and specific needs and tasks to accomplish. In each of these stages, they have specific physical, intellectual, emotional and social capabilities that are quite different from those that they have had or will have at a different age. If we understand the specificity of their needs and abilities, we can then provide the appropriate nurturance and discipline and thus help the child towards healthy resolution of his tasks, towards well-being and healthy development.

For example, a two year old child generally has a very short attention span, approximately 5-10 minutes. If parents don't know that, they might try to read a half-hour story to the child or insist that he play with his blocks for 40 minutes, etc. When he doesn't, and begins to complain or fidget or run off or be distracted or become depressed or start to pull the cat's tail, parents might become angry or frustrated or disappointed or concerned. Their thoughts might leap to ideas of hyperactivity or laziness or improper diet. Somehow their irritability and anxiety and disappointment will transfer themselves to the child and make toxic the air between them. Knowing the facts would help parents structure appropriate activities, have appropriate expectations and feel satisfied about the results and the child. For example, between the ages of approximately 8 months and 3 years, a child has the very difficult task of transversing the separation-individuation phase. He needs to move from feeling totally dependent on the parent for his safety and well-being in the world to a feeling of some autonomy, some safety with himself and his ability to function in the world. Within this large task, there are a variety of more specific, smaller tasks, all phase-specific, crucial to the healthy development of the child. For instance, children of one year of age have no object constancy. If they don't see an object, they assume that the object has disappeared off the face of the earth. Often for a one year old, when the mother leaves for any length of time, he has lost her forever. If he cannot substitute her with another loved, trusted, "safe" person, he will feel abandoned, great terror, lost, a minute away from death. This can be a terrifying experience for a child which can affect the rest of his life. It can, by itself, or with further like experiences, help to keep him forever clinging to some authority figure, not daring to move into authentic individuation and adulthood and autonomous functioning. A patient recalled that she had been visiting a friend in the country. Before the children were awake, the mother had decided to drive over to the supermarket for some milk, leaving my patient in charge. My patient knew the children well and they her, but she hadn't seen them since they had moved to the country some four months previously. When the children, aged 1, 3, and 4, awoke, they immediately ran through the house looking for their mother. Not finding her, they charged, screaming and crying hysterically, onto the freezing lawn in their nightclothes. No matter how hard my patient tried to soothe, comfort and explain, there was no result. There they stood, yelling for their mother until she showed up.

Not all children show their terror and distress in such extreme ways. Some will sit quietly, some will clutch their blankets more resolutely and suck their thumb with more desperation, some will be depressed, some may be virtually unaffected; but for most children, these are negative, far-reaching experiences. If parents understood this, they would not leave their toddlers without making sure that the children knew the substitute parent or sitter and felt comfortable with him or her. They would prepare their children for their going, give plans and time when they would return. They would know to be away a very short time in the beginning, increasing the amount of time as the child seemed more comfortable and able to understand more.

A friend called to say that she had registered her child at a day care center and that the entire week, the child sobbed and screamed when the mother left and had developed nightmares. The director at the school had assured my friend that that was perfectly normal and not to worry. I was appalled at the lack of knowledge and understanding on the part of someone who was supposed to be an early childhood expert. Young children are not manipulative adults. They don't sit down and decide to develop symptoms to elicit behavior from adults. A 3 year old child who is screaming and crying and having nightmares is telling us that he is troubled, scared and distressed. For this particular child, this abrupt separation experience was apparently too difficult and too painful. Indeed, I was very unhappy that such an abrupt separation experience was the norm at this nursery school. At schools that are knowledgeable about children, the entrance into the school experience is staggered. The first couple of days, the parents come and stay while the children play. The next couple of days, they come for half a day, etc., until the child is comfortable in the new environment and with the new teacher. When I was teaching nursery school, I once had a mother sit outside the classroom for 6 weeks. This was a child who had been adopted so that separation experiences were especially difficult for him. After six weeks he was able to let his mother go, and had a wonderful year in school.

There is a great deal to know about the nature, needs and development of children in order for us to be able to help them develop into mature, healthy, loving adults. It is incumbent upon us as parents, teachers, educators, grandparents, therapists to make it our business and our task to gain that information, or we're doing our children a great disservice.

The second great issue in parenting is the personality of the parent. We carry ourselves around, bring ourselves to every situation and not to any situation more than that of parenting. So if we tend to get angry very quickly, we will get angry very quickly at our children. What will it mean for our children to be the receivers of so much and such frequent anger? If we have an unconscious fantasy that we want to be taken care of, we will bring that to our parenting. We will feel resentful at the sacrificing of time, energy and money and, in our specific fashion, we will use our children to fulfill our needs and dreams rather than give them room to grow theirs. Charlotte S. was a successful lawyer with her own firm and a hefty income. She had a constant pinched, pained expression on her face, an eye tic and a sense of being in the wrong world. One of the issues that very quickly emerged was that Charlotte hated lawyering, hated the stress, the games, the one-upmanship, and especially hated the fact that she was living her mother's life, being the lawyer her mother wanted to be and not being the actress she had always dreamt of being. Tom H. worked as a cop. He was constantly terrified of the authority inside and the possible violence outside. His occupation kept him in a constant state of anxiety. But coming from an Irish family of cops, there had been no choice, just an injunction.

We act out most on those closest to us and most helpless, our children. We become to them the parents we hated, the parents we never wanted to be. Ellen R. had a constantly judgmental, intrusive, negative mother who caused her great pain and feelings of worthlessness. She is amazed to see that she has become the same kind of mother to her children. Charles L. never hugged his father and his father never hugged him. Indeed, his father was rarely present. He worked, he hunted, he spent time at the local pub. At home, he was a shadow. Charles L. suffered. He was surprised to learn, in therapy, that he spent 13 minutes a day with his own three children.

Sylvia and Frank P. hated each other, constantly argued and fought and threw bottles and disparaged each other to the children, yet they stayed married. Barry, one of their children, grew up afraid of marriage, afraid of intimacy, afraid of arguing and unable to be loyal, because to be loyal to one person (parent) meant to be disloyal to the other.

In every possible way, who we are and what we are not affects our children, their present and their future and their life. In order to be good parents, we must know ourselves, including our unconscious acting out, understand who we are, what we do and how we need to change to be better and more effective parents. If you're thinking that this kind of knowledge and understanding requires much time, care, money, energy and therapy, you are right. It is a great effort for a great investment, the lives of our children and the society they will make. Parenting is the most responsible thing we do and we must undertake it in the most responsible way possible.

Before the '60s there was, in all our minds, a vision of the family. As we could quickly bring to mind the visual symbol of a triangle, so quickly could we bring to mind the vision of a family as Mommy and Daddy and 2.3 children with Spot, the dog, living in a little white house on Elm Street. Daddy went to work in the morning with his three-piece suit and his briefcase after a peck on the cheek to his wife. Mommy stayed home and efficiently and lovingly, without a hair out of place, ministered to the little ones who climbed trees, swam in the pond and played with the dolls. When Daddy came home, everyone sat around a plentiful dinner table, talking about "their day's adventure," while the Lord smiled in benediction.

Even in those days there were countless single parent families, poor and isolated, and unrelated to the "mythical family." Sarah W.

lived with her mother in a room in someone else's three-bedroom apartment. Her mother was a coat finisher and worked long hours so that Sarah would see her briefly when she returned at night before Sarah went to sleep. Sarah was a holocaust survivor so she had no extended family to speak of and no real roots to connect her to her New Country. She managed mostly on her own, going to school, doing her homework, listening to *The Scarlet Pimpernel* on the radio once a week. On Sundays her mother would take her to a movie house where they would see three movies in a row and come out blinking in what had become the darkness of evening. Sarah read with wonder the stories in the reader of family life, feeling bewildered and confused and very un-American. Three blocks from Sarah's house lived her friend Rhoda. Rhoda had a brother and a sick mother. No father was visible and no one spoke about him. Sarah was afraid to ask Rhoda where her father was, for Rhoda never spoke about him. Rhoda's mother didn't work and Sarah wondered how they managed for money but that, too, she didn't ask because no one spoke about it. She had many questions. The only thing she knew for certain was that Rhoda's family was also not in the American Reader.

Across town and up in Harlem, Martha was trying to manage with seven children of all ages and stages. Martha was black and had never married. The children belonged to various fathers who had long ago come and gone. Theirs was a filthy cluttered one-room apartment where basically everyone tried to say alive for yet another day. Whenever Martha saw *The Donna Reed Show* on a friend's television, she laughed.

Mona and Ike Waterson were farmers in Iowa, working a small family farm. Up at 4:00 a.m., they worked continuously throughout the day. Their five children worked continuously throughout the day. Exhausted and beaten, they hardly spoke to each other. The big event of the family life was father "tying one on" on Saturday night and coming home to rip the house apart.

Irving and Nina Goldberg lived the American Myth. They had traditional roles, the requisite number of children and been brought up from infanthood, knowing what they were expected to achieve. Somewhere along the way, the doubts began to creep in. Nina found out that cooking and cleaning and diapering and getting her hair done once a week were OK, but they often left her feeling lonely and empty and used. When her husband came home and told her about his camera store, she found out that she had better ideas than his for advertising, was much more competent at problem solving and lived more in reality than he. Yet he wouldn't listen to her ideas because she was the housewife and he was the businessman and he wouldn't listen, even after the second store failed. Irving, on the other hand, found himself so exhausted by business problems that he felt wiped out at the end of the day, too tired to have sex, to socialize, to play with his children. He began to wonder what this was about. However, neither one mentioned these feelings, fears and concerns to the other. You didn't talk about it, you didn't doubt it; you didn't question. You lived it. One was Mommy, one was Daddy, and there was family dinner and the end of the day until ten years later when Irving had a nervous breakdown and Nina divorced him.

So for decades, many of us in this country were not living the traditional family, with its traditional roles and rules; many of us secretly knew that it wasn't working. Yet we persisted. We persisted in teaching it to our children and teaching them to strive for it, encouraging them to marry out of high school or to go to college to find a husband. We persisted in idealizing it in books and television, on radio and in magazines, creating an ideal and a myth that was harming us in so many different ways.

It harmed us by taking choice and opportunity away from talented and intelligent women and scripting them into a mold, into which many did not fit, instead of allowing them to blossom into their own individuality. It harmed the men by pushing all the economic burden on them so that they lived and breathed their job and died of heart attacks at 45. It harmed the children because it virtually deprived them of a very important parent, their father, and left them to the mercies of one human being, with no one to protect them from her wrath or her flaws. It harmed us all by putting the decision-making power into the hands of one sex, thus decidedly skewing the fabric of our society. It harmed us by dictating a fixed model when what is most enhancing and most productive are different and viable living arrangements, depending on the needs, desires, wants and resources of the people involved.

In the '70s, it finally dawned on us that these traditional roles, advocated and entrenched as they were in our society, were not productive. Working women found new opportunity, their selfhood, their careers. Of course, they still had their families, their homes, their animals to care for so another myth took hold—the myth of the superwoman. This was a woman who could handle an executive position, be the perfect wife, the perfect mother, the perfect housekeeper, look good, feel good, and be satisfied all the time. In the '80s, '90s and 2000, this myth continues to hold. As it holds, we hear about thousands of latchkey children letting themselves into empty houses, with TV the only company. Other children are suffering through with long days in badly run day care centers or boys' clubs where the options are table hockey or video games. We hear on TV about couples who are having sex once a month because they are too tired to be able to manage anything else. We hear about irresponsibility and absenteeism and irritability in the workplace. A client the other day, whose children are acting out in a variety of ways, told me that of course there was a lot of screaming and dish throwing before the supper hour. Her implication was that this was a normal occurrence in American homes. Indeed, it might be a normal occurrence where parents after a long hard day at work have to drag to a babysitter and day care centers to pick up the children, then push their way home to prepare dinner, see to homework, bath and bedtime rituals, dishwashing, etc. For myself, I remember the few years when I tried to be superwoman. I remember the constant tiredness, the constant irritability and the lack of pleasure in all those activities that I had previously derived so much pleasure from. It is only logical that that will occur. Every human being, no matter how talented and smart, has only 24 hours in her day and only a finite amount of energy. When the hours and the energy are over taxed, depletion sets in.

Because it is impossible to be superwoman, people make accommodations and pretend. Barracudas on the job, they fail to be parents at home. They feed and clothe and house their children, somehow, but they don't listen to their emotional needs; they don't nurture; they don't empathize; they don't support. They're not at the Little League game; they don't remember where the kids' clean pajamas are; they don't know who the latest boyfriend is or why the child is depressed. Or they try to be good parents and let the work slide. Jane was yesterday called three times out of a two-hour meeting by her five year old daughter, Jennifer, who has access to her mother whenever she needs her. Needless to say, the meeting was not very productive for Jane or her company. Tia is a welfare worker who spends as little time as possible on her 30 cases and when you ask her why, she replies unabashedly that her "real work" is her own family. I doubt that Tia's 'cases' are receiving the help or consideration they so badly need. Maria is a teacher in the public school system. She can never stay after school to help a pupil or explain a fraction problem because she has to run five blocks to pick up her waiting children at another school. And so it goes; the workplace suffers.

But perhaps most of all suffer these women who are being told that they should do it all and are suffering, trying to do it all, suffering with exhaustion, with guilt, with headaches, with back pains, with alcoholism, with lack of pleasure and joy, with suicidal depressions, with constant anxiety, chasing a train they can never catch.

It is time to put this myth of the "superwoman" aside, to lay it to rest with the traditional roles myth and to search, with great care and consideration, for new options.

When you ask parents who parent two hours per day how their family is doing, they stare at each other in bewilderment. It's an issue they've never considered. Yes, Billy is failing math and science but that's because he's lazy and 13 years old. Anna is sexually active because of strident peer pressure, and 3 year old Tony doesn't talk because he's spoiled, but they'll grow out of it eventually. They talk about "quality time" and how their children at 4 and 5 are already "independent" and won't that independence stand them in good stead, and they don't consider themselves bad parents, but if they could hear the real loneliness and sadness and rage and resentment and deprivation and longing for closeness in their children that those of us who know how to listen hear, they might. They comfort themselves that they are raising independent children, but independent at what cost—at learning to feel unloved, uncared about and unsupported— just "me" against the world. These children don't make good citizens or good mates or good parents, and these parents are depriving themselves of the joy of true intimacy with their children, of watching and helping them grow and blossom.

Our system of family is not working, and we must look for alternatives that are viable and that will work. What might they be? We might choose to concentrate on our work and not have children. One of the parents might choose to stay home and be the homemaker because they want to or they like it, while the other parent earns the money. They would have to think carefully about the division of work and the need for *combined parenting* and how that could be achieved. Society should consider splitting jobs so that partners can work a full-time job—each sharing part of the responsibility of the job. The results might be beneficial to everyone involved. Employers would get two brains for the price of one and more energetic employees. Husbands and wives could work at their careers and still have a full paycheck, and children would have parents to parent them lovingly and appropriately. Other possible alternatives might be well-run, well-staffed day care centers and afternoon programs on the work site with parents having adequate breaks to visit their children and have their children visit them. Perhaps the government might subsidize homes with young children by allowing part-time household help to do the practical chores, thus lightening the burden of work, physical exhaustion for the family. I don't have all the answers. I only know that those we have found *don't work*. We need to abandon them and very carefully and logically and realistically look for answers that do work. It means that we also need to privately abandon the emphasis on material goods, publicly abandon the emphasis on our military capabilities and look toward the emotional and psychological needs of our families. We need to love ourselves and our children by finding for us and for them lives of quality.

SUCCESS DEFINED AS WEALTH, FAME, CELEBRITY

The Constitution promises us life, liberty and the pursuit of happiness. Happiness in the United States, today, is hardly ever mentioned. What has replaced happiness as the sought-after Holy Grail is success, success defined as wealth, fame and celebrity. One cannot open a popular magazine without seeing some article on "success"—27 Ways to Succeed in the Corporate World; The 10 Most Successful Men in America . . . In an issue of *Bazaar*, Sally Quinn, in an article, once again, on success and failure, talks about her firing as anchorwoman on the *Morning News*. National humiliation! Emotional rejection! Failure! How could I survive? My life was over! Here, a simple firing is construed as devastation. Fame and glory and success—dead.

Don Rickles on *The Tonight Show* describes a social event. "It was a great party. A lot of names were there!" The interchanges, the joy, the life of community evening described in terms of celebrity, success and fame.

Leo Brandy in an article entitled "The Fame and Frenzy of Renown" talks about his youthful aspirations. "We had been nurtured on the central importance of literary fame and New York as the place to get it . . . The conviction was that fame was the only worthwhile thing at all."

For the general American public, success is what it's all about, a lunge after wealth, power and celebrity.

Does success bring with it joy, serenity, peace of mind, happiness? Are "successful" people happy? Marilyn Monroe, Freddie Prinze, Janis Joplin, River Phoenix, Kurt Coburn all had wealth, celebrity and success. They all committed suicide. Mary Tyler Moore, Elizabeth Taylor, Betty Ford, were alcoholics and drug addicts. Karen Carpenter died at the height of her fame from anorexia nervosa. Jane Fonda was bulimic. Boy George, Eric Clapton and McKenzie Phillips were hooked on heroin. Numerous "successful" executives and doctors are alcoholics and cocaine addicts, and myriads of others live lives of emptiness, desperation, sexual addition and violence.

Douglas LaBier, Ph.D., a psychoanalyst who has spent years studying the hidden passions that drive the achiever, in *Modern*

Madness, The Emotional Fallout of Success, talks at great length about "the troubled winners," successful people suffering from boredom or burnout because they have made success in their careers their top priority. What they find eventually is that work cannot give them what they want out of life so they consume aimlessly, discard relationships, harden their hearts and deaden their souls. To quote LeBier directly:

> It may sound crazy to say the successful adjustment
> can result in emotional disturbance but, in fact,
> that's the exact situation that we have in our
> culture. A lot of young careerists find that, as
> they move up, their work requires more and more
> self-betrayal; they tell themselves that their work has
> meaning when it doesn't; they adopt a
> management system that wants not only to
> 'beat' but to kill the competition; they
> pretend they're excited by what they're
> doing when they're not. A lot of people
> just ignore their real values, their
> sense of truth, their sense of integrity
> because to be too aware of these creates
> conflict.

A lot of people put everything into their work because they don't really have an interest in other people. When they shed their work role, they're terrified because they don't know how to relate in any other way. A lot of people just want to be comfortable; they lead lives of desperate comfortableness. And that produces all kinds of aimless consumption—of people as well as objects. Their real love partners are things to be consumed and then thrown out. And all that is done with a kind of deadness. The end result is that human beings don't develop or grow.

In fact, some people are so obsessed with "success" that that is their prime and only target in life. In 1987, the University of California polled 290,000 freshman: 75.6% said that "being very well-off financially" was a top goal, considerably more than in 1986 and nearly twice the 1970 percentage. The interest in developing a "meaningful philosophy of life" had taken a nosedive from 82.9% in

1967 to 39.4% in 1987 [article on "How Feminism Failed," *The New York Times Magazine*, June 26, 1988]. William Newman, a clinical psychologist and stress management expert from Gloucester, Massachusetts, believes that entrepreneurs tend to think of relaxation as a threat to their integrity. "Their whole self-esteem," he says, ". . . depends on constant achievement, which means constantly doing something, which means that a vacation-by definition a time of not doing something—can be a very bad time for them."

Here are the reflections of an "upwardly mobile" seeker. "I, too, believed that I could meet my authentic needs by becoming a corporate projectile, unswervingly pursuing our culture definition of success. Not surprisingly, I have penetrated my share of madness on myself and others."

While the country is busy chasing their elixir of success and finding only the drought of toxicity, men and women are working 12-hour days, having no time for respite or thought or play or joy; children go parentless; manipulation, lying, cheating, greedy grabbing abound as the goal is the essence and not the means. Cars stand outside in rows; televisions abound; clothes closets are packed and the soul is empty.

On October 2, 1988, on a *20/20* segment, the topic discussed was the giving of steroids and body growth hormones to athletes. Interviewed were athletes, coaches, doctors, Olympic officials, and there was a consensus of opinion. It was necessary to give these to athletes because the Russians did so, because competition and success were the name of the game and it little mattered that the administering of these substances were unethical and illegal, that they killed by causing the athletes heart attacks and numerous other health problems. What mattered was the gold medal, however miserably and shabbily grabbed. Having your competitor's knees broken is little enough to do when success is at stake.

Tom Nye has just sold his company for $25 million. He resides in a penthouse on Park Avenue, wears $10,000 suits, plays tennis, dines at Lutéce, vacations all over the world seven times a year. He has just divorced his second wife and is carousing around the globe with a variety of beautiful, nubile young things and some sophisticated older ones. In a journal kept during the nights when he can't sleep, he records his loathing and distrust of everyone he knows, his inability to establish or feel real human contact and his constant obsession with killing his parents.

Marta Hendricks is gorgeous, a goddess and a star. She gets two million a movie, has a husband, a new baby. But Marta is so frightened of losing her success that at the age of 35 she has already had five plastic surgeries. She takes pills to boost her energy when she's working, pills to calm her down when she needs to sleep. She pretends her real estate developer husband is not stealing her money and she spends months away from her baby who calls the nurse Mommy.

Elaine Law has been married for twenty-five years. She has a magnificent home in Rockland county, a housekeeper, four beautiful children who went to Brown, and a handsome husband. Of course, one of the boys is a drug dealer; all of them have no empathy or concern for anyone except themselves. Of course, they don't earn a penny because they look to their mother as the known provider. The husband has had five mistresses in the last three years, openly displaying them in the neighborhood, and the "successful" wife is fifty pounds overweight and cries herself to sleep every night.

I'm not implying that all people who are rich, powerful or successful are empty and miserable. I would guess, however, that for those who are leading meaningful, loving lives, the wealth and the celebrity was inherited, the result of genius or a byproduct of human values. For those who chase the goddesses money and celebrity for the myth of their rewards, they are likely to find ashes rather than rainbows at the end of the road.

When I contemplate success, it ranges in endless varieties of effort and experience. For a shy person to finally be able to make that dreaded, necessary phone call is success. For a hesitant student to raise his grade from 70 to 75 is success. For a parent to have a loving and productive discussion with a child is success. For an actor to move an audience is success. For Carter and Begin and Nasser to have forged the peace treaty is success. For me, success exists on every level, small or large, as long as the individual or group or company or nation has achieved an end truly productive for themselves or others—an end not measured in shekels or celebrity but in growth, development, joy, love, inner satisfaction, increase of necessary function.

Success is authentic. It is not based on falseness, publicity, image-making. Madonna is not successful, regardless of her reputation, because she is not a good or talented actress or a good or talented singer. Yet Kate Johnson, who starred in an obscure off-off-Broadway play, is successful because, through her talent and artistry, she brought magic, joy, insight to an audience, an experience they would not have had had they missed her performance. Success is not Federal Air buying up People Express and New York Air and Transit Air because, though that may put money and power in the pockets of some men, it loses numerous employees' jobs, takes the possibility of flight away from a whole segment of the population and buries the idea of employees sharing in the profits and in the management of their own lines. Success is not a successful advertising campaign but a product that is high in quality and service. Witness these two letters written about GM products:

> The customer seems to have acquired the knack of making its product look good in the driveway but it has had very poor reliability. My 1984 Buick has had 28 problems, half of which I would attribute to poor engineering and the other half to workmanship. My experience is not unique. I have had similar reports from friends and associates.
>
> After 18 months with my poorly engineered, carelessly manufactured and indifferently serviced 1985 Chevrolet Celebrity, GM running an ad campaign saying it is No. 1 in quality would not be convincing.

Success is not a picture of a very attractive, well-dressed, smiling family, with a dog, in front of a large expensive house, when this same family is fraught with disharmony and pain.

Gerry and Allan Smakil lead an upwardly mobile life. They have just moved from an apartment in Brooklyn Heights to a two million dollar home in Great Neck. Gerry is a photographer and Allan is a vice president in a well-known corporation. They have the requisite number of children—2, the dog, the cat, the two cars and the American stamp of success.

When they arrived in my office, each was brutally unhappy. Allan was morose, withdrawn and depressed; no affect was visible. He spoke eerily, slowly, with no strength or conviction. Gerry's affect ranged between enraged and hopeless. She smoked and coughed endlessly and consistently and bitterly complained of overwhelming fatigue. These people had not seen a movie or been to a concert in five months, had not had sex in two months. The older child stuttered, the younger had fits of vomiting of no known physical origin. Even the dog was listless and given to infection.

This outwardly "successful" family was literally killing themselves physically and killing the possibility of joy and love and leisure and discovery and rest and excitement and tenderness in their lives by pursuing the American success dream.

Three years later, Gerry was doing freelance work three afternoons a week at home and painting several morning while the children were at school. Allan had entirely stopped traveling for business and reduced his working schedule to 10-5. They sold the expensive house and moved back to a two-family house in Brooklyn Heights, rented one segment and thus considerably reduced their cash requirements. The elaborate expensive exotic dinners that had once been a part of the yuppie lifestyle changed to salads and chicken and take-out Chinese food with friends in front of the fireplace. The family stopped chasing and relaxed. Social obligation dinners gave way to zoo excursions, skating on the pond with kids or candlelit dinners in Vermont. Antique hunting was postponed for later years and the saved money, time and energy was reflected in the eased burden for the entire family. Gerry stopped smoking. Allan came to life as he began to enjoy life with his wife, his family, playing football with good friends; the baby stopped vomiting.

From the outside, it didn't look good. Gone was the chance of Allan imminently becoming president of the company; gone, for now, was Gerry's opportunity to become another Stieglitz; gone was the gorgeous house and enviable lifestyle . . . but present was being and pleasure and sharing and caring and peace.

For some people of the 1980s, '90s and 2000s, the "success" syndrome has become so pervasive and obsessional that they are unable to even put any leisure or "vacations" in their life. In a *Fortune* article entitled "Power Trips," the author, Nelson W. Aldrich Jr., makes the point that executives fear relaxation and leisure since it interferes with one of their major defenses against powerlessness: constant, consistent and visible achievement. The result is that they don't take vacations or that they translate vacations into arenas of achievement so that Dodge Morgan, owner and publisher of the weekly *Maine Times*, vacations by sailing alone, on a 60-foot sloop, around the world, attempting to circumnavigate the globe in less than 292 days, a winning time in the record book; and Dick Bass of Dallas, founder of Snowbird Ski & Summer Resort in Utah, claims to be the first man to have climbed the tallest mountain on each of the seven continents.

As I'm beginning to write this portion, a program has just appeared on television called *Keys to Success*—the object of the program is to introduce the television audience to a number of millionaires who have made it and who are going to help the audience by giving them tips that will assure the audience's "personal success"—that is, they will help the audience make money. Television shows like *Survivor* and *Big Brother* echo the theme that people will do <u>anything</u> for money—lie, scheme, abandon their children, starve themselves. . .

In any society where there is such a reverence and beautification of success, there is, of course, the primary task of preparing for success. The task often begins as early as 18 months. In the 1960's, Glen Dolman was very popular. He wrote books and articles, appeared on programs, espousing the theory that children be trained and encouraged to use their maximum brain power. In a plan to achieve that, he proposed that mothers and fathers spend a certain number of minutes, several times per day, teaching their 18 months-old baby how to read. For a period of time, this became a touted theory and I personally knew a variety of intelligent parents who dutifully badgered their tots to academic success. Mr. Dolman's book sold very well.

In Margaret Mahler's work *The Psychological Birth of the Human Infant* [p. 10], she speaks of this period of life, 18 months, as one of crucial importance in the development of the human being, as a period of life where the difficult psychological tasks have to be accomplished so that the child may go on to separation-individuation and a healthy autonomous self. The child of this period needs to master within himself the clamoring of the omnipotent control, the extreme periods of separation anxiety, the alteration of demands for closeness and autonomy. Given this period of the child's indecisiveness as to what he wants, his ambivalence about the parent and himself, his fear of loss of love and loss of the object, his continued need for physical activity and his exploration of the world and his age-appropriate cognitive beginning in language to name objects and express desires with specific words, is this on any level an appropriate time to sit this child down and teach him symbols for words he might not even concretely understand? It would take me pages to delineate the possible psychological negative effects of such an undertaking, yet an ignorant neurologist spurred on ignorant parents to this most grievous task so that their children could be "smarter" and more "successful."

When I was teaching nursery school, one day I received an elated call from one of my parents who announced that she and her husband had just come back from celebrating their 4 year old child's "acceptance" into a prestigious nursery school. They were elated since they had heard rumors that in order to gain entrance into this school one had to register one's child at birth, simply for the privilege of an interview. I knew this school very well through a number of different sources. I had observed there for a week during my practice teaching. I had friends whose children were students, and I had met at meetings and conferences with teachers of this school. I knew it to be a perfectly ordinary school, with its share of good and bad points. Yet its reputation and publicity and snobbiness had made it a "successful" school. Now this parent, who had been sincerely unstinting in her praise of me and how much I helped her daughter and fully cognizant of how much her daughter was enjoying her school, was taking her out to fulfill some unconscious need of her own for "achievement" or "success." It came as a great shock and revelation to me, I must admit, that one could so early and so obsessively be concerned with the "achievement" and "success" of one's offspring.

It did not, then, come as a surprise to me to read an article in an issue of *Psychology Today* entitled "The Price of Privilege." The authors of this article, Peter W. Coohson, Jr. and Caroline Hughes Persell, visited 55 boarding schools throughout the United States. They not only administered anonymous questionnaires to 3,000 students, conducted a written survey of approximately 400 teachers from 20 schools, but also spent days at each school, observing and participating in the academic and social life of the school. What they discovered was that the road to 'success' and privilege was littered with negative results, and I quote: "The structure of boarding school life prepares many students for a life of prisoners of their class. After prep school, they will go to the right college, marry right, get the right job, join the right club, travel to the right places and grow weary in the right style. Thus the prep rite of passage creates generations and generations of individuals, many of whom are crippled, rather than empowered by privilege. Again, in our mad dash for success, we are prepared to sacrifice often the autonomy of our children, their individuality and their emotional health." How closely is this article related to LaBier's observations about the 'troubled winners'

And how we sacrifice and manipulate the dash to form our young into 'winner.' In *Nutcracker*, the story of the Schroeder family, we have the mother accepting religious conversion and becoming an Episcopalian so that one of her sons could then attend a prestigious Episcopalian boarding school. Yes, I can hear you say, but she was a mad woman. She was 'mad' only to the extent that she was caught. Many such people are parading our streets, people of total selfishness and no conscience who do whatever they have to to obtain what they 'need' for themselves. It is interesting, in the context of our discussion, that Mrs. Schroeder's 'craziness' was centered around her great investment in money and power. I have heard of people who change their names to get their children into private schools, who borrow money they can ill afford, who invent degrees, backgrounds and connections they never had, who threaten, blackmail and beg all in the name of future privilege.

When I was first married and we would go home to visit my in-laws, somehow the conversation would invariably turn to who had gone to college where. My husband at the time was 25 years old. Most of his friends were in occupations, marrying, making choices about lifestyles. None of this seemed to be of interest. Neither was the political arena, the entire scope of literature, philosophy, art, or local gossip! At the time, I remembered being totally astonished at their single-minded obsession with where one went to college. Now, years later, I recognize it as a symptom of my in-laws' preoccupation with external material success and another example of how society permits the way to its acquisition. College—the right college—the name college—the prestigious college!

Where I grew up in Montreal, Canada, my friends and I went to one of two colleges, McGill University or the, then, Sir George Williams University. At McGill you needed a 75% average to enter, at Sir George a 65% average. Friends of mine ranged anywhere between 65% and 96% in average. They all went to these two schools, all got fairly good grades, a comprehensive education and are all now doing well as responsible, accomplished citizens. There were no interviews necessary for admission, no SAT scores, no letters of autobiography or portfolios certifying to genius. There was only your high school transcript certifying to a nominal amount of knowledge, discipline and capacity to work. When, once, in my twenty year old grandiosity, I complained to the Dean that an entrance level at 65% was too low, he explained to me, with great gentleness and firmness, that it was not possible to judge, by a grade one received at 17, how productive or not one would be in the future, that some people find their subject or niche later in life and, then, take off like a rocket, that the point was to give people a chance and provide them with opportunity. How wise and astute and realistic and humane!

How different to the present system in this country when the myth is that going to a great college—Harvard, Brown—is a passport for life to the "good life." What nonsense. I know a Harvard MBA who works for the IRS at a very lowly job with a very lowly salary. I know another who is a cocaine addict. I know two Yale graduates who run an electric shock mill which makes them rich but is barbaric for their patients. I know three Yale graduates who are literally starving actors, unable to get a job. I know a graduate from the University of Virginia who has no morals or scruples of any kind but would do anything and hurt anyone he needed to achieve his own selfish ends. The kindest man I ever knew who had great success at rehabilitating drug-addicted adolescents graduated from an obscure college in Kansas. And then, of course, we all know of multimillionaires who never graduated high school. And of course we also know of 'successful' people, graduates of famous universities, who at university lost not only their virginity but their souls. The point is that the university is a place to learn, to grow, to develop, in intellect, character, autonomy, direction, spirituality and humanity, not a success mill. But that is how we view them, and we torture our children so that they can gain

41

entrance. We shove them into expensive preparation programs where they learn 'tricks' to take SATs; we buy them professional help to prepare their portfolios. We write, if we have the talent, their autobiographies. We push them and they push themselves into activities and social community works in which they have no interest and for which they have no talent so that they will have 'credits' that look good on their college applications. We take away their telephones and their friends so that they can make the 90s they need to enter the hallowed halls. To what purpose?

What magical gift lies waiting there? Perhaps some association on some level to class and privilege, whatever that means. Certainly not excellence. My best friend's daughter attends Oberlin, a prestigious college of the humanities and the arts. I am appalled at the lack of control over curriculum choices so that a true thorough liberal education is practically impossible and not impressed at the level at which courses are taught, nor the interest or concern for the individual student or his development as a person or scholar. Her friends attend Harvard and Brown and Amherst and Yale and Oberlin. I wish I could say that I was gratified by their literacy or curiosity or interest in humanity or their exploration of the meaning of life. Mostly, they consider what bar they will go to, what rock group they want to hear or what career they can pursue so that they will have enough money to live in Manhattan. No, my daughter and her friends are not a crass group of unthinking yuppies. They are intelligent, beloved children of liberal homes who are products of the society they live in and the schools they go to.

Our emphasis is on the wrong syllable. We need to desist adhering to the myth of the name and become concerned with the general question of what is excellence in education, of how one arranged for the schooling that will help our children bloom, each in his individual way, in his unique way, into authentic, loving, productive people, emotionally, intellectually and spiritually whole, and how to offer this excellence to all our young people since all deserve the best possible opportunity. For example, we teach our children higher calculus and the life of the Sanwans. However, we teach them nothing about the inner workings of their psyche, about relationships, about parenting—the essential issues of a person's life beyond making a living. College students can traverse complicated majors with honors without having any courses in politics, economics and government and emerge into a voting adulthood with very little understanding of the foundations or process of government of their country. Beyond excellence in instruction and a quest for excellence in performance, we need to address the questions of what makes a decent, honest, loving, well-functioning person and citizen and how do we educate for that. It is only in thoroughly and specifically addressing the above question in all its multi-levels that we can possibly turn this society around from a narcissistic, empty, destructive one to one of health. The Greeks wanted a 'healthy mind in a healthy body.' They knew whereof they spoke. It would not be a bad motto to follow, much more productive than teaching to grab more money, a bigger desk, greater power.

Does training for success cease and desist after college? Of course not. There is graduate school and horrible laboring and sacrifices for PhDs and then, in the real world, there are Dale Carnegie courses that teach you to speak in public and be 'personable' so that you can achieve success. There are consulting firms and consultants who teach you how to 'dress for success,' how to change your 'image' so that you will be more 'successful.' There are speech classes to take away your 'regional' accent and bring you that much closer to 'success' as if you could not possibly manage to be vice president while speaking with a Southern accent. There are the right restaurants to be seen in and the right health club to join. And so it goes. One expert recommends walking over coals shouting "Win! Win!" to bring out the hidden winning streak in our character. Others suggest that we try to succeed "100% of the time and that we reach for success." One success expert shows slides of his possessions during lectures and says, "This is my Mercedes 560SEL; you can have one like it. This is my ski condo in Aspen; you can have one like it. This is my million-dollar house in Santa Barbara, and the only thing stopping you from having one is yourself." We buy books like *Winning Through Intimidation*—which basically espoused any possible method as long as the 'top' was reached.

What this training has achieved for us, in my estimation, is a country wildly pursuing success and money, and a generation of hard-driven men—and now, women—overachievers willing to sacrifice almost anything and anyone in the name of career success.

How do I define 'success'? Firstly, for me, it's not a desperate search for money or power. In early childhood, and the ages of one and two, the critical separation-individuation stage, children of depriving, dictatorial parents, especially, and those of loving parents as well, experience themselves on some level as powerless and empty with all the good stuff, supplies, residing in the parent; the good stuff includes love, attention, comforting, maternal things, the power to protect and make secure. I see our society's love affair with power and money as a group of adults arrested at that narcissistic, early childhood level of powerlessness and emptiness, chasing the supplies they feel they don't have, didn't get and need in order to survive. Yes, I see our pursuit of 'success' as a pathological symptom or defense. Healthy 'success' has no one definition. Everybody has his own definition, depending on his priorities, so that one person may consider himself successful if he achieves his goal of living a life of saintly poverty, another if he feels good about himself and his way of life, another if he saves two minority high school students from dropping out, another if he breaks the three-minute mile. And we should broaden our definition of success and recognize a much larger spectrum of 'success,' depending on striving, doing and achieving, so that a young man who finally succeeds in overcoming his shyness and anxiety to venture into the world of heterosexual relationships is considered as 'successful' as one who has just made the football team. Finally, it seems to me that the successful life is a synthesis in which personal happiness, family life, career, money, concern for one's fellow man, fun and pleasure are balanced rather than sacrificed one for the other.

Most importantly, let us stop writing books on 'success' and writing articles picking out the 50 most successful people in the world. Let us stop letting other, outside people judge us as to our accomplishments and the quality of our lives. That, too, is a narcissistic characteristic of needing for one's self-esteem the approval of the parent or authority figure. Let us take the time and energy to look inside ourselves, to discover, from ourselves, what authentically makes us happy and to pursue that with diligence, to be successful, then, in the eyes of the person who matters most, ourselves.

There used to be a slogan that Elizabeth Taylor was the most beautiful woman in the world. I remember being constantly incensed by that because, though I considered Ms. Taylor most lovely and feminine and sensuous, I could conceive of millions of women of different types, coloring, height, etc. who were in their own unique fashion equally beautiful, feminine and sensuous. And so, with success, it comes in many sizes, shapes, qualities and varieties. Let us appreciate it and value them all. We have the right to determine for ourselves the kind of life we deem successful, and not let Big Brother—in the shape of government, our parents, the corporation, the media, the self-help gurus or any organization—determine the standards by which we measure the success of our lives.

> None think the great unhappy but the
> great. —Young

> Nothing makes a man so cross as success.
> —Trollope

> Perched on the loftiest throne in the
> world, we are still sitting on our own
> behind. —Montague

> A man must (as the books on success say)
> give 'his best,' and what a small part of
> a man his 'best' is. His second or third
> best is often much better. —Chesterton

> The slave has but one master. The
> ambitious man has as many as can help in
> making his fortune. —LaBruyére

> Nothing is enough to the man for whom
> enough is too little. —Epicurus

> Everybody wants to "be" somebody: nobody
> wants to "grow." —Goethe

> It is often the failure who is the pioneer
> in new lands, new undertakings, and new
> forms of expression. —Hoffer

MYTHS ABOUT AMERICA

Sitting at a country pool this morning, I watched a toddler party in progress. Mothers, and fathers too, were playing with beautiful babies in the water, giggling and nurturing, splashing and rejoicing, landscape proof of what Hillary Clinton had announced in a recent speech on television—that America loves it's children! Last week, at an Arts Award dinner in New York State, former Governor Cuomo re-emphasized the importance of family and mutuality within the family, members of the family caring and sharing with each other.

In my office, a mother told me that her three year old daughter was the most important thing in her life, and another mother told me that she would find a way to bring her child in from New Jersey to Manhattan every week if I felt it was necessary for his proper development and mental health. This was a pregnant mother, poor and already burdened by three other children.

On television I heard a variety of celebrities exhort our youngsters not to give in to drugs. Judith Wallerstein appeared once more to discuss the necessity of couples staying together, and a husband and wife team announced the formation of a new magazine to be freely distributed to parents that would deal with all the various ages and stages of childhood and help parents to understand what was needed for the well-being of their growing child.

Indeed, wherever one looks, it appears that, in America, we love our children and we care about their growth and development.

However, *The Editorial Research Report* published in 1985 by the Congressional Quarterly Inc. reports the following:

Child psychologist David Elkind states that "today's child has become the unwilling, unintended victim of overwhelming stress—the stress born of rapid, bewildering social change and consistently abusing expectations."

Dr. C. Tibson Drenn from Springwood Psychiatric Center in Leeding, Vermont reports that "parents use their children as tools in the battle with the Joneses. Children are judged, not on the basis of their self-worth but on their grades, extra-curricular activities and college acceptance and their career goals. The abysmal experience of being average with super-achieving parents puts enormous pressure on a teenager. The goals a parent has for him are often so high that anything he can do will never measure up."

Tom Cottle, a Harvard University psychologist, suggests that American parents give their children love on the contingency plan, on the bonus plan. "I really think it's important for you to achieve and when you do, "I'll think about loving you." It should be love no matter what."

Edward Weaver, Director of the American Public Welfare Association, remarks that parents value children but they value other things as well, such as material goals, status and their careers. Given these conflicts, they neglect their children and don't give them a fair shake.

Current research shows that 1% of female adolescents (about 1 out of every 100 females between 10 and 20 years old) have anorexia nervosa. The average child spends 12,000 hours in the classroom and 18,000 hours watching TV. In 1994, 57% of babies born to white teenagers and 92% of babies born to black teenagers were illegitimate.

Department of Health and Human Services statistics:

28% of the nation's tenth and twelfth graders are problem drinkers. 8% of adolescents between 12 and 17 years of age currently use marijuana.

According to the Senate Subcommittee on Juvenile Justice, approximately one million children a year escape from their problems by running away from home.

It is believed that there are 600,000 child prostitutes in the nation. 4,493 youths under 24 committed suicide in 1997. Most people believe that there are three times as many as that statistic. In 1997, 1,700 children under 18 were implicated in committing 1400 murders. In 1998, there were 1,135,000 divorces, leaving millions of children living with one parent. There are nearly 5 million latchkey children.

In 1997, The U.S. Department of Health and Human Services reported 1,941,253 official reports of child abuse and neglect involving over 2.7 million children.

In 1977, persons under 18 accounted for 10% of the murders, 17% of the rapes, 32% of the robberies and 52% of the burglaries.

In 1977, according to the Uniform Crime Reports, 1.8 million wives were beaten by husbands. Over 1 million children are abused each year, physically, sexually and through neglect. Professor Muarry

A. Straws of the University of New Hampshire said at a 1978 meeting of the American Psychologist Association: "The American family is the most physically violent group or institution except for the police or military."

How do we then reconcile this tragic, dismal set of statistics with the idea that, in America, we love our children? How, then, do we explain this paradox of espoused love for our Children and these bitter facts? From my perspective, the idea that we truly love our children is one more myth, one more story, we tell ourselves about ourselves that is not true. Love is exhibited by behavior. How do we behave towards our children? The very same President Reagan who espoused the priority of children announced proposed regulations concerning work rules for children 14-15 years of age. They would be allowed to work until 9 o'clock on school nights, until 10 o'clock on non-school nights. Work would be expanded to four days a week; prohibition against certain types of work would be lifted. Thomas Donahue, the secretary treasurer of the AFL-CIO, said the regulations would create a pool of cheap part-time child labor, the beneficiaries of which would be the various individuals that already have notorious records for violating and undercutting fair labor practices. No one believed that the beneficiaries would be the children.

In a society where there are nearly 5 million latchkey children, a government-sponsored comprehensive day care-after-school care plan is still unavailable. Social health and day care services that were available to low-income families are being scaled back or eliminated. Good government-sponsored day care services that would provide relief to working mothers, and healthy physical social development for children, might bring large portions of the welfare ranks into the ranks of the employed, might prevent juvenile delinquency, drug abuse. Yet it is not to be. In 1973 [*We the American Woman*, Beth Millstein, Jeanne Bodin, Science Research Assoc.], when nearly 1/3 of all mothers with preschool children and ½ of the mothers with older children were working outside the home, often to keep their families above poverty level, when 41% of our children were completely dependent on the earnings of women, President Nixon vetoed the comprehensive Child Development Act which provided for the development of child care facilities in the United States, free to some and on an increasing fee scale to others. He gave as his reason that he wanted a family-centered approach to child care rather than a communal approach. It is interesting to watch President Nixon creating his own myth of a family-centered home while the reality is that in many homes, the family is not present or available for much of the time and the life of the child.

In the 1987 *Statistical Abstract of the United States* issued by the Department of Commerce, Bureau of Census, under social welfare [p. 345], where sources of funds for public programs are listed, there is no category for day care. In the 1984 Census, as reported by the 1987 *Reader's Digest Almanac*, only 14% of employed mothers with children under 5 had their children in day care centers. What happened to the other 86%? Were they all so wealthy that they could afford private governesses? Of course not. What this statistic explains is that there are so few government-run day care centers in the United States that they can service only 14% of the population. And do the private companies, the big and middle-sized conglomerates who make profit by the billions every year, fill the gap and provide well-organized, well-staffed, appropriately nurturing centers for the children of their employees? Sociologists and psychologists argue that this would ensure higher productivity among employees, at much profit to the company, that this would ensure peace of mind for parents who could feel assured of the welfare of their children and who could even visit them at lunchtime or on their coffee break. They argue that this type of arrangement would prove greatly beneficial to the mental health of the children who need to be reassured of the presence of their parents. Yet the private sector has not responded. A very few companies have provided these facilities. Most have not. Their shortsightedness and lack of concern for their employees and the health of the growing generation of this country's citizens is only equaled by their inability to move themselves from their self-serving, money-hoarding position.

What about the older latchkey children, the grammar school-aged children, the ones who have to return to empty homes after school where there is only a television to keep them company? Have we provided for them? Some philanthropic agencies—like the Jewish Philanthropies, the Boy's Club of America, Children's Aid, Catholic Charities—are doing what they can, but no government monies are being spent on uniform, productive, imaginative, caring after-school programs for our latchkey children. We leave them there, lonely, alone, forgotten and capable of doing emotional and physical harm to themselves.

Do we treat them with love when we have them in school? We shove them, 35, into a room, diverse, unique individuals different in intelligence, background, culture, and we ask one underpaid teacher to teach them, to be responsive to their individual differences, needs and capabilities. This teacher has to take a polyglot people, thrown together from every ethnic strain and culture in the world, and give it a common body of symbols to serve for both communication and cohesion. Impossible. And who are the teachers? Do we ask our teachers to have psychological evaluation so that we can see if they are loving enough, healthy enough to teach our young? Do we require them to have, as psychoanalysts are required to have, their own therapy so that they can work through their personality problems and not project them on their innocent students? Do we provide them with enough classes in child development, in ways to spot pathology, in methods of teaching that will reinforce the strength of our children and deal productively with their weaknesses? No.

And then, we proceed to pay them a starting salary of $30,000, an unbelievable salary in a city like New York, while their classmates who have chosen law and medicine and computers, within the first few years, are making $75,000 to $80,000 a year. It is a wonder that not many of our best and brightest and most creative young people are choosing education as a career?

Several months ago, I had occasion to go see the guidance counselor at my daughter's school. This is a public high school for gifted and talented children, a school touted for it's uniqueness in the country's system. This man, a capable and caring one, was nevertheless the sole counselor that day, in a school that services 2000 children. I was there for five hours, attempting to obtain some uninterrupted time with him and watching him literally try to roller-skate his way through this impossible job. I didn't know whether to laugh or cry. Several colleagues who have similar jobs, and who I know to be caring and competent people, shrug their shoulders hopelessly and say that having to spend one or two days servicing an entire school leaves you with the possibility of doing nothing but completing the mounds of paperwork. Another acquaintance, not quite so concerned, has a different perspective. When I inquired how she can handle such a taxing job and still see clients in the evening, she responded, "Oh, that job is just a way of making money. I don't do anything there."

A report by a teachers' group in New York City points out that an "average of three children in each class will sooner or later require institutional care because of emotional and mental breakdown but the education budget allows three minutes of guidance per child during the entire term."

A shocking percent of the school plant is run down, its equipment archaic, the classrooms overcrowded and underheated, the textbooks out of date. In other schools, the degree of vandalism and drug abuse and truancy is so prevalent that the students can't simply walk around their school but must obtain passes to go in the simplest direction. Many schools have virtually become high security prisons with school guards on constant watch. The Columbine High School incident is a tragic example of how little attention we pay to the needs and lives of our children.

As for the quality of the elementary and secondary education, I quote the noted professor and scholar Mark Lerner, who in his book *American Civilization* has this to say:

> Much of elementary and secondary schooling
> is little more than assembly line processing
> with mechanized teaching methods and an
> intellectual level rarely rising above
> mediocrity. Since American power rests on its
> technology, the trend has been toward the
> technical and the vocational with little
> stress on the capacity to handle general ideas
> and sift irrational from rational. Given the
> boredom of high school pupils and the pull of
> jobs and spending power, it has been found in
> some big-city school systems to weight the
> high school curriculum toward the vocational
> in order to keep the boys in school a few
> years longer. While this helps produce
> skilled manpower, it ignores the fact that the
> problems which will make or break America are
> no longer technological but social and cultural.
> It also ignores the intellectual, spiritual and

> emotional, social and cultural needs of the
> Individual students. [p. 737]

In 1997, the United States spent, for education, 22 billion dollars. In the same year the United States spent 276.7 billion dollars on the military, and nearly 9.2 billion dollars in aid to developing countries. It seems we love and value much more the development of other countries than we do that of our own young.

In the same year, America spent approximately 93.8 billion dollars on amusement and recreation services, 63 billion on motion pictures and 7.2 billion on video tape rentals.

In 1999, an acknowledged 20% of youngsters between the ages of 12 and 17 use drugs, and 23.3% currently use alcohol. In 1997 there were only 10,867 alcohol and drug treatment programs, and only a fraction of the government's money is being spent to address the problem. What are we really doing to save the lives and futures of our children? We are marking shopping bags with slogans that enjoin us to "say no to drugs"; we are having quick spots on television where well-known personalities are exhorting young people to say no to drugs. We are trying to solve a complex, multi-determined problem with Madison Avenue techniques.

One young person, (under 24 years old), every 1 hour and 57.0 minutes killed themselves in 1997. They found the world so ugly and difficult, themselves so angry or hopeless, that they have cut off their lives and their futures. It is most likely that since many suicide attempts are not reported, the numbers may be twice or even three times as high as those admitted in the published reports. As of 1994, there were only 607 hotlines for youngsters in this severe emotional difficulty.

It is estimated that one million children runaway from home each year. They are running out of pain, trauma, suffering, confusion, helplessness, hope. Many of them end up dead, many of them end up prostituting their bodies in the street, many of them end up criminals. In New York City, there is one center, Covenant House-privately funded, which valiantly attempts to keep these runaways on a temporary basis and attempts to turn them around from despair and destruction to hope. But as one dedicated worker, frustrated and distraught, proclaimed on TV: "What are we to do with them? Most of their homes are too awful to return to and we have nowhere to put them, nowhere to send them for help and rehabilitation, so we clean them up, give them a place to rest, and then most of them return to the hell of the streets."

In 1997, there was nearly one million substantiated victims of child abuse, 1,077 of these children died; millions of youngsters are sexually abused by someone known to them in a parenting role. In 1994, 2.5 million children lived in the sole custody of a drug-abusing person. In 1988, there was an estimated 354,000 child-snatching cases in which the parent took the child with no intent to petition for legal custody. There is little that can be done by the enactment of the Parent Kidnapping Preventive Act. In these cases, the parent is left to hire a private investigator or to investigate on his own. Substantial government help is unattainable.

How is it, then, that we say we love our children and then expose them to devastating, non-productive, humiliating experiences in broken-down schools with dead and empty curriculums, incompetent or uncaring or overwhelming and overwhelmed teachers? How is it, then, that we say we love our children and allow them to wander around lost and alone on streets and in empty homes? How is it, then, that we say we love our children and then allow them to runaway into nothingness, into drugs, into crime, into oblivion? The answer is that we don't love our children, that this espoused love for our children is an institutionalized myth, a story we tell ourselves about reality when the reality is that we as a nation, as a country, behave like a self-centered, self-serving, abusive and neglectful parent who, to save his own comfort, energy and money and to stave off his own guilt, denies the reality and pretends the problem does not exist and then, when no longer able to pretend that the problem does not exist, pretends that it can be solved without great effort or great expense of money and spirit. In making ourselves "comfortable," we are demeaning our children.

On to another American institutionalized myth: that of equality.

Ostensibly, one of the touchstones of the American philosophy is equality. In the Constitution, we assert that "all men are created equal" and are endowed by their creator with the inalienable right to life, liberty and the pursuit of happiness.

We are born—not equally. We all recognize that there is a difference between being born in Harlem Hospital, in a stick hut in Puerto Rico or in a private room in New York University Medical

Center. From the beginning there is little equality in the surroundings of birth. In the hospital wards there is a hierarchy of solicitude for mother and child depending on income. There is no equality of education. People who can afford it send their children to the hallowed halls of private school, others to public school. Even public schools differ. In Nassau county, $11,204 was spent per pupil in 1990; in Westchester, $11,867 was spent per pupil in 1990; in 1999, in metropolitan New York City alone, only $8,616 per pupil was spent. In a study done in 1980, it was revealed that only 2.6% of the white population had less than five years of schooling. However, 9.2% of the Black population (4 times that number) and 15.3% of the Hispanic population (5 times that number) had less than five years of schooling. In the years of growth, the conditions that make for an expanding personality—adequate medical care, a chance for recreation and travel, access to sun and sea, music and art and books—must be paid for and many of us cannot pay for them. Some of us are intelligent and talented but we cannot go to college, our parents can't afford it. Scholarship aid fails to solve the problem since it rarely covers living expenses, nor does it fill the gap of the earning power in the family income, and scholarships are becoming more and more rare. To borrow money in Federal loans is either not to be able to cover your costs and expenses or to tie yourself to the yolk of unbelievable debt. Young people have meager starting salaries. One of my patients, after paying his living expenses and his college loan, had $10.00 a week for miscellaneous expenses. Public colleges keep raising their tuition fees so consistently that they've become accessible mainly to the middle class alone.

In 1986, the U.S. Conference of Mayors reported, at its annual meeting in Washington, that many persons were hungry and homeless in American cities and that the causes were unemployment, scarcity of low-income housing, low welfare payments, high standards for food stamp eligibility. There was a 28% increase in demand for emergency food and a 25% increase in demand for shelter during the past years. Seventeen percent of the demands for food went unmet and shelters in the city had been forced to turn away individuals for lack of room. There is, of course, no economic equality. Is there racial equality? Certainly, there is no economic racial equality. In 1997, [U.S. Census Bureau, *Statistical Abstract of the United States, The National Data Book, 119 Edition, 1991*], 11% of White families were living below the poverty level. In Black families, 26.5% were living below poverty level and 27.1% of Hispanic families were below poverty level. There are approximately two and a half times more Black and Hispanic starving people than White starving people. According to the 1998 U.S. Census, the median income of a White family is $40,912, that of a Black family is $25,351. Of the 1,159,700 businesses owned in New York State. in 1992, only 50,601 were owned by Hispanics and 51,312 were owned by Blacks. In 1987, 9% of the executives in this country lost their job; 50% of those were Black. Certainly, the concept of social racial equality is desirable, according to our philosophy, but according to our reality, non-existent. Stewart Alsop in *The Center—People and Power in Political Washington* [Harper & Row, N.Y. Evanston & London, p. 25] writes:

> Most of White Washington goes about its
> business hardly aware that Black
> Washington exists. And with White
> Washington, the awareness often takes the
> form of fear. Crime rate in Washington
> is appalling, more than 90% committed by
> Negroes, mostly against Negroes—but most
> white householders keep arms in the house
> and elaborate burglar systems. . . Most
> of the business and most of the real
> estate in Black Washington are owned by
> White Washington . . . (There is nothing
> new in this.) For a long time, the White
> majority made life miserable for the
> city's Black minority. Before the Civil
> War, slaves made up a useful portion of
> the city's revenues. "If they wish to
> live here," wrote a contemporary quoted
> by Constance McLaughlin Green, ". . .
> let them become subordinates or laborers as
> nature has designated." In Franklin
> Roosevelt's day and even after the war,
> Washington was a strictly segregated
> Southern city.

Not all that much has changed. Even though school segregation is officially, by law, not permitted in this United States, there are still areas where schools continue to be segregated and, where they are not segregated by choice, they are segregated by circumstances—e.g., when a school is 90% black because it is in a black residential area, this school will most likely receive far less money per pupil than one in a predominantly white neighborhood. According to American law, housing discrimination is prohibited, but we all know that it exists, that there are neighborhoods in every city in this country that continue to discriminate against populations that are not white Protestant Anglo-Saxon middle class. Even in mortality the races are not equal. Average life expectancy for a white woman is 3.5 more years than that for a black woman and average life expectancy for a white male is 4.5 years more than for a black male. I wonder how other inequalities unite to form this outcome.

The Klu Klux Klan and the Neo Nazi Party are not the only lunatic fringe embodiment of anti-Semitic, anti-Black feelings prevalent in the under=strata of this country. Remember that, in the whole history of this country, there has not been a President, or Vice President, who has been Jewish, Hispanic or Black, and it was only after some 200 years, and because he had an infinite amount of money at his behest, that a Roman Catholic succeeded in become President. Will Joe Lieberman be successful in breaking that taboo and, at what cost? However, in 1991, David Duke, the former leader of the Klu Klux Klan, was a serious candidate for Presidential Office. In the whole spectrum of American arts and culture, the Black and the Spanish have been ignored. Even in the present, there are only three TV shows which star Black actors, none which are Hispanic. Those shows and movies that are in evidence very seldom reveal the true Black experience or Hispanic one. Recently, a movie was made—*Hollywood Shuffle*—by an actor who was no longer able to contain his frustration and pain about the difficulty of obtaining any honorable acting, directing or producing work for a Black in this country. When I search my mind for well-known Black or Hispanic-American writers or symphony conductors or song writers, only a very few spring to mind. Why? Are we discussing here a genetic difference in intelligence and talent, as was suggested some years ago by a well-known psychologist? No, we are discussing a paucity of opportunity and inequality at every level. And it is important to remember that, in spite of the fact that "equality" is supposedly a major prong of our philosophical belief and adherence, the Black and the Jew also have had to fight for what they have achieved every step of the way. To win a measure of civil rights, to wrest a better education, to gain a foothold in politics, they have had to march and lobby and go to jail and sit-in and die and be helped by two world wars, the march of industrialization, their massed purchasing power and the Supremacy of Federal law on matters of civil rights. Whatever there is, and there is much further to go, came by the toil and sweat of the brow and not by gift.

Neither is there equality between men women. The Bureau of Labor Statistics provides the following figures for 1999: In the same level managerial positions, women made $675.00 a week; men made $943.00 a week. In the same level technical sales or administrative support position, women earned $430.00 per week, men earned $631.00 per week. Women who were factory operators and laborers made $332.00, men in the same position earned $473.00 per week. Women earned 70% of men's earnings for the same job at the same level. The median earning for a full-time worker who was 15 years and older was $13,703 for a woman and $25,212 for a man in 1997.

Unequal as these conditions are, we have to remember that women, like Blacks and Jews and Hispanics and Irish, had still to fight long and hard to achieve even this. A country which blazes "equality" in neon in its code handed not equality to the women of America. First there was the suffrage revolution as part of the hard-fought movement for equal rights in which a succession of strong-minded women, in the face of jeers and humiliation, won the vote, broke into previously barred professions and eked out the right to an equal education with men, to speak in public, to hold office. Second, there was the sexual revolution, directed against the double standard of morality and aimed to get for women some of the same privileges of sexual expression that the men had forever. Third, came the revolution of manners with women, shedding their cumbersome garments and adopting form-fitting clothes and revealing swimsuits and shorts, taking part in sports, driving cars, piloting planes, smoking and drinking in public. Fourth, there was the kitchen revolution, with mechanized kitchens and canned and prepared foods, giving some women greater leisure and enabling some to get jobs. Finally, there was the job revolution which transformed the American working force as it also transformed women's role in the economy. In 1963, a series of measures were enacted to eliminate discrimination of women in industry—the Equal Pay Act. However, employers very cleverly soon found measures to circumvent the law, such as giving equal jobs dissimilar titles—calling a male an "executive" and a women in the same position an "executive assistant." In the 1970 Census, in spite of all of this law, females who had finished high school earned only 56% of the amount earned by men of equivalent age and education. Working women with four years college earned 55% of the median amount earned by college-educated men—$7,930.00 as opposed to $13,370.00

In 1965, came the Civil Rights Act, a bill primarily against race discrimination. Eighty-one year old Howard Smith of Virginia opposed this bill vehemently and, wishing to halt its passage, added a provision outlawing "sex discrimination." Once again, women were not being accorded respect for their rights and needs but being used by men for their own purposes. Ironically, the bill passed. However, once again, employers were able to circumvent and ignore the law. Women were not "strong" enough for jobs, couldn't carry, wouldn't "do well" in a predominantly male atmosphere, etc. Very recently, an employment manager of a private personnel agency was chuckling to himself as he enumerated to me the 104 ways that were available to him of "getting around" the Civil Rights Act against sex discrimination in employment.

In 1972, the Equal Employment Opportunity Act was passed which extended the prohibition of discrimination based on sex to federal, state and local government as well as to educational institutions. So effective are these laws that only 1% of high level civil service jobs were held by women. These were a succession of self-liberating movements, movements generated and fought for by women, movements that need to continue to accelerate as the aspired-for equality is yet a distant dream. We have not been able to pass the ERA, we have to be ever-vigilant or our pro-choice rights and we are, in every way, not "equal." For many in America, women's equality is unimportant, dangerous or peripheral. As Henry Kissinger said in 1973, "For me, women are only amusing, a hobby. No one spends too much time on a hobby."

Even now, few women are directors of big corporations; few women form government policy; few women are owners of press and media, and even those who are powerful in their ownership of wealth are functionless with respect to their wealth because they lack the strategic control of it.

In a recent study of married couples in which both partners hold similar level executive positions, it was discovered that in three out of four marriages, the wife was also responsible for the caring of the children and the running of the household. While the man in this society is specialized to making a living, the woman, even if she too has a career, is asked to be both specialized and unspecialized, to be at once worker, sexual partner, mother, home manager, hostess, nurse, shopper, figure of glamour, supervisor of the children's schooling and play and trips, culture organizer and Carrier and charity worker. In many ways, in reality, psychically and socially, the woman still exist in a society dominated by masculine power and standards. In a *Demographic Profile*, a portrait of New York City from the 1980 Census issued by the City of New York, Department of City Planning, we realize the following statistics. In the Bronx, of 100% of the population of families with children below 18, male householders alone with children are 1.3% of the population, while female householders alone with children are 24% of the population. In Manhattan, male householders alone with children under 18 are 1.3% of the population, women are 16.7%. In Staten Island, male householders alone with children under 18 are 1% of the population, women are 18%. Is this equality?

Every day on television, we are bombarded by myriads of products designed for women, promising to make her sexy, desirable, glamorous, coveted. In all this myth of equality, we don't designate men and women as equal partners attempting to form loving relationships with each other. The woman is conceived of as the huntress; the man, the hunted. She adorns herself, perfumes herself, sets herself in places she would not ordinarily be, manipulates and pretends, all to capture that elusive pair of pants. The arts of advertising and salesmanship lose no chance for encouraging her. If the American woman were in danger of forgetting for a moment about clothes and cosmetics, lingerie and nylons, deodorants and perfumes, the advertisers make sure that doesn't happen. "If you believe in one great love as many people do, then you should wear Jontue," "Find a touch of romance at many department stores," "The Maidenform woman has the winning touch," exhort the merchandisers. In a Cherry

Seven-Up commercial, all the people are in black and white except a beautiful couple bedecked in the pink of fairy tale and romance. He and she are different because they are both drinking Cherry Seven-Up. . However, she is more different than he since she is drinking diet Seven-Up and he is drinking regular. Subtle but ever-present is the concept that it is the woman who has to do the slaving and the suffering to make herself appealing to the male, who then decides whether he will buy her or not. After she has grabbed her man, the media then portrays her as housewife and mother. No other roles are open to her. Women are rarely seen selling major products. In *Superman IV*, I was appalled to see the supposedly intelligent, intrepid, feisty Lois Lane simpering at Superman: she knew that "whatever he did would be right" . . . that "it didn't matter how much time he spent with her—even a few minutes was enough" . . . agitating over whether the duck she was preparing for him would be basted for perfection. Suddenly, this supposed saga of partnership had converted itself into the American male fantasy—a simpering woman who cooks and takes care of you, allows you to do whatever you want and, throughout, tells you how wonderful you are. The American male wants not an intelligent, equal partner with wants, rights and needs but a geisha tap dancing on eggshells, striving to ascertain and fulfill her man's (master's) every desire. In John Updike's *The Witches of Eastwick*, the author, with supreme craft and irony, portrays the American male-female scene. The man is charming and sexy and pursuant and the female, in order to get him and/or sex, must be accommodating and subservient to his needs. If one (female) attempts to be assertive, self-loving, self-protective, one ends up without a man.

Is it equality not to pass the ERA amendment? Is it equality to invent bogus, specialized myths about the ERA which have nothing to do with reality? The opponents of ERA argue that a passage of this bill would require women to be drafted. Firstly, we have a volunteer army, not a drafted one. If that were to change, exemptions for family responsibility would be generally extended. Other than that, with rights come responsibilities. If men can fight, so can women. If men can die, so can women. The opponents of ERA argue that ERA will force women to work outside the home because men will no longer need to support their families. In truth, no such requirement, need or regulation is embodied in the ERA. The Era, according to some, will end segregated facilities such as public restrooms and school locker rooms. The ERA does not invalidate an American's right to privacy and does not have this intent. Other myths associated with the ERA are that a woman's place is in the home, that women are not seriously attached to the labor force and that they work only for extra pocket money. The reality is that more than half of all women between the ages of 18 and 64 are in the labor force where they are making a substantial contribution to the nation's economy. In 1973, of the 34 million women in the labor force, more than half were working because of pressing economic need. Women are out ill more than male workers, say the pundits. They cost a company more. A recent Public Health Service study shows little difference in the absentee rate due to illness and injury, 5.9 days a year for women compared with 5.2 days for men. Another illusion harbored by many Americans is that women don't work as long or as regularly as their male co-workers; their training is costly and largely wasted. The reality is that the average woman worker has a worklife expectancy of 25 years as compared with 43 years for the average male. However, single women average 45 years in the labor force. "Married women take jobs away from men," scream the indignant. In 1972, there were 19.8 million married women in the labor force. In that same year, the number of unemployed men was 2.5 million. If all the women stayed home and unemployed men replaced them, there would continue to be 17.3 million unfilled jobs. Moreover, most unemployed men do not have the education or the skill to qualities for many of the jobs held by women.

"The employment of mothers lead to juvenile delinquency," press the opponents of the ERA. Studies show that multiple factors must be considered as causes of juvenile delinquency. Whether a mother is employed outside the home does not appear to be a determining factor. In all my years of working with children and in the experience of my colleagues, a mother working outside the home was never a principal or sole factor in the formation of a child's emotional problems.

"Men don't like to work for women supervisors," says the detractors. In a survey in which 41% of the reporting firms indicated that they hired women executives, none rated their performance as unsatisfactory. Fifty percent of the firms' male executives judged women as adequate, 42% of the male executives judged women as the same as their predecessors in the job and 8% of the male executives judged the women executives to be better than their male predecessors.

As of this date, equality for women in the form of the ERA has not yet been accomplished. Myth and inequality persist.

Nor does there exist equality before the law. In recent published statistics, it was printed that in divorce cases, many of them precipitated, engineered and desired by the male, the woman is virtually annihilated. Generally, after a divorce, a man's standard of living rises 32% and a woman's drops by 72%. Many of these woman, unnecessarily, become poverty statistics.

Sally R. is a very pretty, intelligent nurse in her 40s with three children aged 9 to 18. One night, when she came home from work, she found her lawyer husband packing a suitcase. Without warning and with no discussion or preparation of any kind, he informed her that he was leaving. He had found a woman "who could really make him happy." With that, he showed her a picture of himself and a naked blonde in a bathtub and, as if that were not enough, he left, with the picture, a steamy poem he had written to his new girlfriend. In shock, terror and incredible pain, the astonished Sally tore it up and threw out the evidence. Several months later, when absolutely no support had been forthcoming for herself and the children, Sally hired a lawyer. She subsequently discovered that her lawyer husband, in preparation for this move, had manipulated the system in such a manner that it was impossible to prove his net worth or his real income. He had started new corporations every year, eliminating the old so no proof was available, had hidden monies she knew not where and was presently reporting an income of $28,000 per year. This was a man who, she knew for certain, was making $200,000 per year. With no money of her own, the mediocre lawyer she hired could do nothing for her. After seven years of wrangling in the courts, she emerged with a nominal sum of child support and $15,000 for her for the rest of her life, period.

Dorothy L.'s husband, by his own admission, abandoned her and their four school-aged children and was living with another woman. He installed a wiretap on his wife's telephone and for two or three months would go into the basement of his wife's home to collect tapes of his wife's conversations. Nothing incriminating was said by the beleagured woman. However, the husband had his own plan.

Before the trial, he went through the tapes, cut them and strung pieces of sentences together to achieve sentences like "I feel so guilty." The court allowed this tape to be played, against strenuous objections by Dorothy's lawyer, even though the judge knew what happened and himself called it a 'composite' tape. Following the judgment, the wife was left with too little money to afford the cost of an appeal to seek a reversal.

In *Every Woman's Legal Guide* [Barbara A. Burnett, Esq., Consulting Editor, Doubleday & Co., Inc., Garden City, NY, p. 351], the point is made very clearly that judges in divorce cases have considerable discretion in making awards of property between ex-spouses, that most judges are male and that the record is very clear that many share sexist assumptions with the rest of society and apply these in court. In California, a community property state, a woman and her husband shared equal ownership of a ten year old construction business. The wife was the force behind the success of the company, and also its company president. Her husband, a carpenter, played only a minor part in management. The judge, observing that construction is a male-dominated industry and overlooking her role in the company, ordered her to sell her half of the company to her husband. The negotiations went badly and she received far less than her interest was worth. She was able to find another job in construction and had to start her own firm all over again.

Linda L. is a beautiful, intelligent, statuesque woman who for eight years had run the home and entertained her husband's business guests. One day, without any warning, he left the house, cut off the charge cards and withdrew all the money from the joint bank account. When Linda emerged from her unbelieving stupor, she discovered that she had two dollars to her name. For three days she starved until she finally overcame her humiliation and borrowed some money from a friend. Linda is a very talented playwright but it is not a profession which afforded her much money. With no income of her own, she was forced to go to a legal aid lawyer while her husband, who was making $180,000 a year, hired a $275.00-an-hour attorney. Needless to say, with the disparity of attorneys and with an older male judge, Linda emerged from the divorce proceedings with a total sum of $15,000-no alimony, health benefits, etc.—only $15,000 for eight years of love, affection, sex, laundry, cooking, cleaning, entertaining.

These women are not unique, not examples of misjudgment on their part or especially bad representation, but merely typical of the treatment that our system affords women under the law.

There are only eight community property states [*A Woman's Legal Guide to Separation and Divorce in the Fifty States*, p. 4], where legal title or possession of or right to property acquired during the marriage is provided and where both husband and wife have an equal claim. In other states, the starting point is that everything is the husband's and that he has the duty to take care of the family. While all states have passed laws specifically enabling a woman to hold property, most states don't permit her to convey the property without the husband's consent. Title to personal property is often placed in the husband's name by tradition or for business reasons. Even when the laws are fairer and less discriminatory against women, rules and laws are often ignored to rescue the husband.

In rape cases, the law requires supportive evidence such as presence of semen, physical injury or a witness [*Every Woman's Legal Guide*, p. 435]. The strictest laws require corroboration of all parts of a rape victim's statement. This is not true for other crimes. The result of this inequality before the law is that prosecutors may not take a case to trial without material, corroborative evidence even though the facts are that often there is no corroborative evidence because there are no witnesses, men do not always ejaculate, women wash themselves . . . Also, traditionally, the law has allowed a woman's prior history to be introduced as evidence to question her credibility and to infer that, because she consented to sex in the past, she may have also consented this time. Rape shield statutes—laws forbidding such questioning—have been passed in some states but not in all. It is important and interesting to note that the alleged rapist's criminal record *must not* be brought out at the trial. Given this circumstance, judges and juries might make decisions based on a woman's sexual experience rather than on the incident itself, *or* the perpetrator's prior criminal record. Historically, the law has required a woman to have "resisted to the utmost" in order to be able to make the charge of rape. Again this requirement is not necessary for other crimes. Some states no longer require physical resistance, and personal injury is no longer needed as proof. Nonetheless, a woman must show that she did not acquiesce, that the act was accomplished with force or threat of force. The fact is that rape is a life-threatening situation. If the victim resists, she can be killed; if she does not resist, in an attempt to save her life, a charge of rape can often not be brought. Most state laws do not recognize forced sexual intercourse as rape when partners are married. These laws often apply even when unmarried persons cohabitate. Although some states have revised the law, in others the law is limited to cases in which the couple had a written separation agreement or a court order to live apart. The effect of such laws or lack of them is to encourage in men the belief that they have a right to rape their wife, and it makes the police hesitant to answer such emergency calls regarding marital rape, reasoning that this is a domestic matter that should be handled privately, and the fact is that many women report being repeatedly and brutally raped by their husbands.

In prostitution cases, only the prostitutes are brought before the law, although this is a situation where clearly two people are involved in breaking the law. In spite of the fact that a 'John' law exists in New York City which would rectify the above disparity, it is much more honored in the breach than in the execution.

Although women are unequal before the law, persecuted by the law and by the lack of law, there are other minority groups in the United States which have *no* laws to provide for them. There is no federal legislation yet passed banning discrimination in housing, employment, public accommodation and commercial space on the basis of sexual orientation. Consensual homosexual activity, which was a crime in every state until 1962, still is a criminal act in 25 states [*Human Services & The Gay And Lesbian Population of New York* by Donna Tapper and Mignov Saubar, Community Council of Greater New York, March 1986]. It is these laws which label homosexual practices as a crime that are considered to be the basis for discrimination in employment, child custody disputes and other areas of life. Certain social institutions such as marriage and family have historically been defined as relationships between men and women, and legal rights have flowered from these definitions. Because a gay couple is not recognized as legal, one partner has no right to the property of the other, as does a spouse. Survivor benefits are not available to the surviving partner in a gay relationship. Gays, unlike marrieds, have to have specific legal contracts to ensure that the partner is beneficiary of the property or is involved with necessary health care decisions. Indeed, gays and lesbians are not only unequal before the law, they are unequal in multitudinous aspects of our American life. As reported in a study (above) on human services to gays and lesbians, although New York's diversity incorporates a tolerance of different lifestyles and customs, homosexuality remains a subject of controversy and a target of prejudice. Gay organizations are largely supported by privately raised funds, using volunteer service organizations. Except for services to persons with AIDS, there are few illustrations in the city of mainstream providers that have designated programs for, or make special efforts at outreach, to gay people [p. 45].

What is bad in this regard in New York City is worse elsewhere. In Minneapolis, for example, it was not until 1974 that community pressure led the United Way to provide funds for a gay staff person at Minneapolis Family and Children's Services to provide services half-time on a "loaned" basis to Gay Community Services of Minneapolis. Currently, only two staff members are assigned full-time to the program while two others work half-time with other cases. To provide only this minimal service, workshops and retraining and reprogramming sessions needed to be held for the staff of this organization to help them tolerate the population they were serving. Prejudice and intolerance run deep and far, and equality is far behind.

Neither, in America, is there equality for the aged. In our culture, it seems natural for us to treat the old like the tag end of what was once good material. It seems difficult for man or woman in our culture to see that a man who has ceased to be a hustler or a woman who has ceased to be a beauty may have deepened internally and that the urgencies of life and living may have given way to something of deeper value. The most flattering thing we can say to an older American is that he "doesn't look his age" and "doesn't act his age," as if it were the most damning thing in the world to look old. There is little of calm self-acceptance, of self-valuing, of feeling 'equal' or 'just as good' among the old, or the building of the resources which give inner serenity and may compel an outer acceptance.

There is correspondingly little in the culture of valuing of old people. The Japanese revere their ancestors; the Chinese set values on the qualities of the old; the Canadians provide financially for the economic and medical needs of the old. Since the Americans, however, have been taught to value success and have been taught that success belongs to push and youth, it is hard to revere those who no longer possess either. To build a code of conduct toward the old requires not only personal kindness but generations of the practice of values from which the old are not excluded. Where there are few codes of honor, it is impossible to have a code that will pay honor to the old.

Instead, we damn them with myths, misperceptions, misconception and a practical lack of caring and help. In *Successful Aging* [Robert and Ruby Neuhaus, John Wiley & Sons, New York, Toronto, etc.], the authors delineate both the myths of aging and the realities. We begin with the concept that after 65, everyone goes steadily downhill. That is simply not so. People age differently and many people don't show any unusual aging defects until much later [p. 17]. In a Duke University longitudinal study, more than 50% of people over age 65 had no detectable deterioration in their physical condition and more than 50% of the people polled rated their health as "good"! Another false assumption is that old people are pretty much alike. To the contrary, as a person grows older, there is a concentration of his uniqueness as a result of his varied and special life experiences. "Old people have it easy" is a floating rumor. Indeed, old people have to deal with poverty, fear of crime, lack of transportation bodily decline, loss of prestige, and the death of loved ones. Households with heads of household over 65 years old experienced over 25 million household crimes and more than a million personal crimes. Low income for the elderly is a harrowing fact [*op.cit.,p.23*]. According to the U.S. Census Bureau, in 1998, 3.4 million elderly lived below the poverty level. Eight percent of the aged received incomes under $5,000 and 28% received between $5,000 and $9,999. For families with heads of households 65 and over the median income was $31,568, ($32,3298 for Whites, $22,102 for African Americans, and $21,935 for Hispanics). Social Security is the chief source of income for 18% of the aged population. For retirees 62 and over, the average monthly Social Security benefit amounted to $804.00 for individuals and $1,034.00 for couples.

With crime and many other problems come also problems of medical care. Studies have found that elderly patients are treated in emergency rooms with less patience than younger people [By *Youth Possessed—The Denial of Age* in America, by Victoria Secunda, The Bobbs Merril Co., Indianapolis, New York, p. 150]. With physicians, there is a lack of prestige associated with geriatric specialty. Many physicians are impatient with older people and incorrectly blame the aging process for a variety of symptoms instead of providing a thorough exploration of the problem. On the other extreme, the elderly are overmedicated, have perfectly ordinary mental health symptoms described as senility and left untreated. Most elderly people, unfortunately, find the high cost of health care, even such health care, prohibitive. In the hospital, Medicare will not pay for telephones, radios, private duty nurses, private rooms, doctors' services, nor will it cover custodial care. In the home, Medicare will not pay for full-time nursing care, nor for custodial care, nor for drugs, nor for homemaker services. Medicare will not pay for doctor services such as routine medical examinations, routine foot care, eye and hearing examinations, eyeglasses, hearing aids, immunization, false teeth or orthopedic shoes.

In fact, in our society, life for the older generation is anything but 'easy' or 'fine' or 'equal.'

A most common myth is that for the older generation, the passionate days and nights of sex are memories of the past. Not true at all. Individuals possess the capacity for sexual intercourse up to and beyond the eighty year level.

The dictum that people should retire at 65 is totally erroneous. The findings are that of people over 65 who stay in the work force, three million or 13% have a 20% better absentee record, are slightly more productive and have fewer accidents than the younger employees.

These myths, these inequalities and discriminations against the older generation permeate our social fabric. Dr. Richard Blumental [By *Youth Possessed*, p. 14], an associate researcher scientist at New York State Psychiatric Institute, states that the reason that people are obsessed with looking and staying young is that everything we read in the media about being old isn't very nice. Our culture is essentially a denial of old age. In 1983 Caldwell Davis Partners advertising agency [*By Youth Possessed*, p. 72] did a study of age perception that showed that even a product targeted for the older buyer uses older models at its peril. When George Kennedy, 50, advertised Tums, the sales were mediocre. As soon as he was replaced with a younger actor, the sales piled up. Helena Rubinstein's "Beauty doesn't have to end at 50" attracted 60 year olds rather than 50 year olds and was restructured. Ad companies feel that they have to "talk to the younger person inside the older consumer" and thus dominant models are between the ages of 18 and 29 and less than 2% of models are in their 60s.

People knowledgeable in the business world readily admit, though often incognito, that older people at agencies and companies are systematically eliminated. Indeed, many companies have a cut-off date of 40 for insurance coverage. The problem became so acute that an organization had to be formed, the Forty-Plus Club, to help find jobs for middle-aged executives. Placement people acknowledge that, contrary to discrimination laws, companies ask to hire only young people, whether secretaries or executives, and plastic surgery is becoming common for middle-aged executives who want to continue to function. Forty percent of Americans report that they were forced to retire and no one seems concerned that the highest suicide rate is among recently retired men of over 65. Arthur Miller's *Death of a Salesman* continues to stand in today's reality.

What business and advertising decrees, media perpetuates—so that we will hear *Time* tell us [*By Youth Possessed*, p. 83] that Charles Aznavour "still" looks great at 58. Mick Jagger is an aging but *still energetic courtesan. The New York Times* will tell us that ad executive Philip B. Dusenbugett is now 47 but still young at heart and, in a 1983 *Fortune* ad, we read that "it's nice to make it while you're young enough to enjoy it," leaving no doubt that success and joy and fun are only for the young.

Everywhere, we are giving our senior citizens the message that they are bound to a system that has no place for them, that has no empathy for them and that does not value who they are. Immediately, the message must be reversed, because the attitudes toward ageism influence the perceptions of the self and the concomitant behavior of its victims and reinforce in the elderly negative attitudes and ambivalent feelings. Immediately we must abandon the myths and live in the reality. Beauty comes in every shape and form and age. I have a 67 year old woman patient who, with grey hair and no make-up and with very simple clothes, is in form and aspect and expression quite beautiful. No one who had seen or spoken to 92 year old Martha Graham will deny that she was beautiful or that 88 year old Cary Grant was beautiful before he died or that Georgia O'Keeffe was scintillating and exciting to the end or that my dance instructor's mother was elegantly radiant and magnificent at 92 and on ad infinitum. Indeed, many people become more beautiful and more handsome as they grow into their body and the years of living and loving and wisdom seep into their bones. In our modern age, with our understanding of exercise and nutrition and the importance of good medical care, there is no reason why we shouldn't have an entire generation of handsome, spry 80 year olds dancing their way into the future. I am convinced that my 83 year old mother has more energy than I do.

The substantive facts are that colleges and universities are finding that many older students are doing better than their younger classmates [*By Youth Possessed*, p. 27], that Bernstein and Stokowski and Graham and Fosse and Wilder and Miller and Williams and O'Keeffe and Hepburn and de Koonig created and are creating and performed with as much as or more skill, passion and virtuosity and magic than ever. In 1983, John Russell wrote in *The New York Times* [p. 59], "George McNeil was seventy-five years old this week, but you would never know it from his recent paintings. They are in every sense wild paintings, wild in color, wild in the power of the paint, wild in the acrobatics that he imposes upon the human body and .wild in the high humor of his observation of everyday life."

A friend of mine who recently passed away, Michael Loew, was 75 years old when he won the Guggenheim Award and he painted the most luminous, magnificent paintings almost until the day he died and had the most child-like wonder about the world imaginable. Elderly people have wonders to offer us. Let us not fritter them away.

We need to understand that senior citizens have accumulated a lifetime of experience and understanding and expertise and knowledge about themselves and the world that the 30 year old may not have and we need to reconsider such issues as mandatory retirement or hiring policies that draw the boundary at the 40th birthday. We must find and make available to our elderly means and methods where they can continue to feel useful and needed in our society and where we can benefit from their considerable largesse. Whether they continue in their careers or become consultants or continue education or devote themselves to charitable organizations or hard-won leisure and pleasurable activities, we must honor their contributions and respect their efforts. Shakespeare said, "The fault . . . is not in our stars, but in ourselves." The fault is not in them but in us and our prejudices and infantile misconceptions. I remember with sadness an 86 year old woman in a synagogue in which I was a member. Unbowed and undaunted, with red hair flying, she not only donated considerable money to the synagogue, but time and energy as well. She was ever there, to usher in people during the services, to set up the collation, to run the bazaars. Never, while I was there three years, was she elected to an office or in any other fashion honored or even verbally appreciated. Yet the 35 year old blonde who came to decorate the succah received, from the rabbi, public and unending accolades. In a society where we so often esteem the glitz without the substance, it may be time to esteem the substance without the glitz.

Practically, what the elderly need is a social security system commensurate with the standards of the day, quality medical services, access to individual and group therapy, recreation and interest groups, quality housing arrangements, quality nursing homes for those who need them, appropriate transportation, protection from crime. To achieve these aims, we can learn from other countries. In Sweden, there exists a policy of gradual retirement. In 1982, a program was initiated which allowed workers between 60 and 65 to slowly cut down their work hours and receive government payments to make up for the lost income. Employers pay an extra payroll tax to finance this program. In Denmark, there are voluntary social services provided by the government. They are offered to the citizens as a 'right.' Institutions are provided as homes for older citizens. The rooms in these institutions have locks on doors, a privilege not permitted in American nursing homes. They are found in the center of the community with easy access to public transportation. Most residents have their own rooms with their own gardening plots if they desired them. In the United States, 1.6 million elderly people lived in institutions in 1997. There is considerable confusion here about the various types of facilities. There are complex admission procedures and plans for financing care for the elderly people that lay people find hard to decipher. The waiting period to get into a nursing home may be from three months to three years. For the vast majority, there is a severe lack of quality in this institution care. Nursing care is limited and is often thought of as merely custodial. The needs of the elderly to receive social, psychological and other meaningful therapeutic services are ignored. Aides are poorly trained, ill-equipped for the positions they are in, and abuses are common. In other countries work with the elderly is a sought after occupation. In Sweden, there are 923 helpers per 100,000 people; in Norway, 840, in the United States,

28.7. The Danish finance the elderly with home care as long as possible and then, if ever necessary, with institutional care. There is no stigma in the Scandinavian countries, Japan, etc. attached to advancing years and no negative value placed on being a senior citizen.

It is this that we have to strive for in this country, a method of providing dignity, both emotional and practical, for our elderly people so that they can be a riches both to themselves and to us. As Walt Whitman says in *Leaves of Grass*: Youth, large, lusty, loving-youth full of grace, force and fascination, Do you know that old age may come after you with equal grace, force, fascination?

In an article in the *Washington Post* [May 29, 1986], Tad Squic, who visited Sweden, Denmark and Finland to evaluate and understand their treatment of the aged, explains:

> The Scandinavians call their approach
> "open old age care." This means that
> older men and women are encouraged and
> helped to live their mature years in
> dignity in their own homes instead of
> being "warehoused" in nursing homes.
> There are a variety of programs that
> allow the elderly to live safely alone,
> receiving outside professional help when
> needed or in sheltered communities that
> provide stimulating activities.
>
> Firstly, there are "home helpers," paid
> workers who come to the homes of those
> aged who live alone and assume chores
> that the elderly can no longer cope with.
> They do housekeeping, cleaning, shopping,
> cooking, running errands. These helpers
> are trained and paid by local;
> municipalities and are considered to be
> municipal employees. When the main and
> urgent tasks of life are provided for,
> the older person is then free to occupy
> him-herself with reading, piano playing,

studying, learning new skills,
socializing. Indeed, sometimes, healthy
old people are mobilized to look after
the less fortunate elderly and are often
paid for their services.

Safety in individual apartments and in
the "sheltered villages" (where the
elderly live side by side, offering each
other companionship) is assured by state-
of-the-art alarm devices that connect
each elderly person living alone with an
emergency center. There are telephones,
alarm bells on walls and devices that
attach to a person's body. These
emergency centers offer not only quick
medical help and monitoring and
supervision but also needed words of
support and reassurance to a depressed
person. For these people, there are also
community centers available where they
have dance classes, language classes,
weaving instruction, lounges for
socializing and cheap meals. In the
"integrated housing projects" where the
elderly live side by side with young
people and their families, social centers
exist complete with library, wood
workshops, photo labs, saunas,
gymnasiums, tennis courts, as well as a
hospital for uses of the apartments.
Here the old are surrounded all the time
and rejuvenated by the young people and
children.

These programs in the Scandinavian
countries are paid for by the government
and supported by all the leaders of the
countries, even the conservative leaders.

As Mauno Kovito, the president of
Finland, explains, "Old People must be
maintained active, self-reliant and free."
There is a consensus that society is
responsible for the elderly citizens and
for helping them to live with dignity.

According to the 1998 U.S. Census, there were 8,787,832
Americans over the age of 80. People 65 years and older are projected
to be 20% of the population by 2030. Our life spans have been
advanced and extended to new limits. Our estimated life expectancy is
greater than it has ever been: 76.7 years. The Census Bureau has
recently warned that "the rapidly expanding numbers of older people
represent a social phenomenon without historical precedent." Yet,
while the Scandinavians and others have been developing their new
strategies for the last decade, the tendency in the United States has
been to preserve the obsolete tradition of isolating people in nursing
homes or hospitals or just letting them fester as burdens on their
families, fearful, depressed, helpless, and often targets of physical
abuse. We cannot allow that to continue to exist.

MYTHS ABOUT PSYCHOTHERAPY

She was tiny and plump and curly-haired and twelve years old. Her parents had brought her to me because she had suddenly started to have horrendous nightmares and was refusing to leave the house. She sat in a chair across from me, rigid and obviously terrified, staring at me with large brown eyes. She had difficulty speaking, answered in hesitant monosyllables, and every time there was an impulse of any part of her body to motion, she consciously halted it. Finally, after about half an hour of painful groping on both our parts, she blurted out, "Why are you asking me these questions?" "Because I'm trying to understand something about the problem, something about you." "But you can read my mind," she exclaimed. "You don't have to ask questions." And then it emerged that she knew that I, as a therapist, could read her mind, that she was in a panic about what I might discover and was thus making a conscious, desperate attempt to control herself and her body as much as she could. My memory immediately went back to when I was in sixth grade and we were told that our biology teacher would be replaced for several weeks by a graduate student is psychology. I remembered how, on the first day of his tenure, I, too, had attempted to be a statue in order not to allow him access to my mind, my thoughts, my inner being. This, however, is not a phenomenon common to 11 and 12 year olds. Many people feel that the therapist has magical powers, magical powers to read the mind, magical powers to fix the problems, magical powers to stop the symptoms, magical powers to heal the illness.

That, of course, is not the case. If a therapist is intelligent, well-trained, sensitive, empathic, responsible and in reasonable emotional health, he or she will be able to offer a partnership to a patient in which, together, they will explore the problems and *together* will arrive at insights and understanding about the patient, the problem and ways to help the patient lead a more productive life. There is nothing magical about the process. It is often difficult; it is often time-consuming; it is often expensive. Like any process, it can move forward quickly and with startling results while, at other times, the mining is arduous and halting; or, at times, it can bog down altogether in the mire of stasis. One is never certain where one is going, or how or when one will get there. Therapy requires a degree of trust, patience, commitment, struggle for both the patient and the therapist in the doing.

I can understand how people reading this might be overwhelmed by the hugeness of the task and experience a sense of hopelessness about the work that might lead to avoidance of and rationalization against the need for treatment. One of our most common rationalizations and another myth is the idea that treatment is only for "crazy" people. When questioned as to the definition of crazy, people are often vague and confused, murmuring phrases about people who can't function in society, people who think they are Napoleon, people like "Son of Sam", the derelicts of the Bowery. They might not be certain of the definition, but they know that it is not they.

As a middle-aged person who has been working with people, in one capacity or another, for most of my life and who has been a psychotherapist for at least 25 years, I am convinced, beyond a shadow of a doubt, that therapy is not only for the societal fringes but a necessity for all of us functioning, proud people. I equate the care of our psyche, our emotional health, with the care of our body, our physical health. Just as we don't seek treatment for only the more extreme illnesses of AIDS and cancer and heart attacks but, hopefully, get regular physical checkups, educate ourselves as to methods preventive of illness and attend to our backaches, diabetes, colitis, flus, etc., so we must educate ourselves to the prevention and prompt attention of emotional illness, which can range from very specific symptoms like headaches, unexplainable by organic origins, to alcoholism, depression, drug addiction, relationship problems, feelings of worthlessness and emptiness, psychopathy, inability to deal with success and on and on through the varying symptoms and disorders and ranges of emotional health. Unattended, these emotional illnesses cause havoc in the person, in the family and in the body politic, as evident in our statistics on alcoholism, child abuse, wife battery, drug addiction, teenage promiscuity, runaways, suicide, homelessness, divorce. A recent film, *Fatal Attraction*, beyond its entertainment value, makes a very telling and poignant point about our society: that often—just beneath the "normal" mask of a charming, intelligent, supposedly functional human being—can be an emotional illness, a 'crazy' core that is a clear and present danger to ourselves and to those with whom we come in contact. *Prince of Tides* makes a similar point in another guise. Most of us are not as seriously disturbed as the unfortunate persons in these films, but many of us are that to a lesser or greater degree and, in not attending to our problems, we hurt ourselves and skew our lives and hurt and skew the lives of those we come in contact with—often, those we most profess to love.

To be good to ourselves and the ones we touch, we must take our illnesses and disorders into the consulting room. To do that, we must give up, as individuals and as a nation, the myth that we are an emotionally healthy people, a myth belied by every present statistic, and begin to educate ourselves and our fellow citizens to the nature of mental illness, to its manifestations, to its causes, to its consequences, to the potential for prevention and its treatment.

Another myth that we espouse in relation to treatment is that it's not effective. It does not help. It does not change people. Time and again, I have heard people say, "He's been in therapy for ten years and it hasn't done him any good. He's as crazy as ever" . . . "They went to couple counseling and they got a divorce anyway" . . . "The psychiatrist released him and said that he was cured, and then he went home and chopped up his whole family" . . . "Therapy is only good for the therapists. It makes them rich and everyone else poor" . . . "You don't need to pay someone to listen to you. I have good friends. I tell them my problems. They listen" . . . "Therapy changes your personality. It takes away your talent, your creativity. It makes you into another person." The people who make these statements believe them and, in some cases, they might even be true, but they say nothing about the truth and reality of expert therapeutic intervention.

Yes, Virginia, there are people who have been in therapy for ten years and have made very few concrete gains or progress in their lives. They may even be able to spout the nature of their disorder, recall past memories connected with their difficulties, express feelings about past significant others, but they are unable to apply this knowledge in the service of the ego, to feel better, to like themselves better or to be more productive. There may be various reasons for this. It is possible that these people, who seem on the surface the same, have changed in subtle, invisible ways, not apparent to the naked eye. It is possible that change for these people is very slow and their pace must be respected. It is also very possible that they have been working with an incompetent therapist who doesn't know how to do the work. Work with a competent therapist will, after some time, produce important, productive changes in one's personality and one's life.

Couple counseling or marriage counseling does not have as its only aim 'fixing the relationship.' Of course, the first hope and attempt is that people will examine their situation, learn where the problems are, learn to eliminate them, learn to deal better with them or learn how to accept them. However, what sometimes emerges is that the relationship is not salvageable, that it is too dead or too empty or the people too locked in mutual war or hatred to be untangled. In that case, a wise marriage counselor will work towards an understanding, a peaceful resolution of unfinished business, so that each individual may be allowed to proceed with his or her life rather than remain stagnant in an untenable situation.

Psychiatry, psychology and social work are not exact sciences. It is possible, after considerable study and exploration, to understand the personality dynamics of a human being and to have a very good idea as to how he might behave in various circumstances. It is not possible to make *exact* predictions about how he will behave. Psychiatrists and mental health professionals need to be very careful in their discharge planning. Unfortunately, too many of us are grandiose, irresponsible, avalanched with an overwhelming amount of work. This is not an excuse for unnecessary murders but an explanation that mistakes, poor judgment, irresponsible people say nothing about the need for or efficacy of treatment.

In all my own work and knowledge of the work of my peers, treatment has never caused the loss of talent or creativity. To the contrary, it frees and opens the personality to freer and more spontaneous work and greater capabilities and possibilities.

In some cities and with some people, fees are exorbitant and treatment may be hard to come by or impossible to come by for people who don't have the means. I make no apologies for those of my colleagues who charge exorbitant fees. I don't, for a moment, buy their rationalizations that high fees will make the therapy more valuable to the patient, that he will make greater strides, that this will be an incentive for him or her to earn money. I believe high fees are, generally, in the greedy, grandiose, self-serving interests of the particular practitioner. Some therapists will tell you that their fees are a healthy recognition of the time, money and energy that they invested in the pursuit of their profession and of their work. For me, that proposition leaves out two important elements—one is that the central purpose of our profession is to help people. How can we help people who cannot afford to see us? We, then, become an elitists class working with an elitist class.

There are therapists who understand this and have lower fees, have a sliding scale, dependent on the income of the patient. There are therapists who make themselves available as clinicians and supervisors at clinics where rates are more affordable. Find one of those therapists or one of those clinics. Hopefully, they will provide for you the help and counseling and understanding you need. Hopefully, as a nation, we will establish a national health program where therapy is recognized as crucial and is provided for and made available to all who want it and need it regardless of their monetary status.

Henry R. is dapper and handsome and bright, an up and coming entertainment lawyer who meets and pals around with the rich and famous and jets casually around the world. He has enough money to live very well and a wife and children and a family. Yet Henry is constantly restless and bored and depressed. He attempts to still the dissatisfaction with relentless activity, eighteen-hour days and sex of every unsavory variety. But the persistent emptiness inside him can't be filled and he is a desperately unhappy man on the way to the next thrill, hurting himself and those he touches.

Philip L. is tall and movie-star handsome and quite successful in his career. He has two children whom he prizes and whom he tries to see as often as possible. Philip L. is clear on the fact that, in spite of his successful societal stance, he feels worthless and inadequate and unloved because his parents were unable to offer him either verbal or physical affection. What he is unaware of is that he is equally unable to offer any real, consistent nurturance, support, caring, affection to the many and various females he beds, and that, while consciously desperate for a meaningful, affection-laden relationship, he is unconsciously making that impossible through his hatred and distrust of women and through his use of them as supply objects rather than as equal, entitled humans, and that he is providing for the children he "loves" the same distant, withholding presence he experienced in his family of origin.

Ann P. is a very pretty, intelligent, self-supporting, responsible, charming and playful woman. Yet she is continually depressed, frustrated, confused, dismayed and powerless. This lovely woman is unable to create a productive life for herself because she is run by an unconscious fantasy that someone out there—God, a man, men—will make her life for her. Her life will magically organize itself so that she will feel happy and live happily ever after. Having delivered her life, part and parcel, into the hands of others (whoever that Other may be at the moment), she has abdicated responsibility so she does not explore herself for what she wants or how she can get it and, simply, waits.

Bonnie S. had a hysterical mother who was terrified of the world and expected that the worse would happen; indeed, the worst was just around the corner. To this day, 70 year old Bonnie can't have a cold without feeling that it's really a manifestation of the AIDS virus, even though there is no realistic way that she can possibly have AIDS. Every possibly happy event, like the marriage of her grandchild, is accompanied by feelings of impending doom and gloom, and most good and joyous and affirmative life events are experienced as "not good enough" or, somehow, maligned. It is possible to imagine the stress and unhappiness and frustration and self-blame and hopelessness that accompany this world view and that visit Bonnie and those with whom she connects.

Robert T.'s mother died when he was two months old and he was raised by a tyrannical, belligerent, schizoid father, incapable of love or empathy or understanding, only capable of abusing the other and bending him to his will. The rage of such a father was enormous but Robert could not afford to vent his own rage. That was not possible with such a father who might have been capable of murdering an oppositional child. It was further impossible because, as a child, Robert could not survive alone, only through his father—to have labeled his father as "bad" could have been to virtually have left himself alone, unprotected, to have rendered himself dead—and so he repressed the rage and turned a lot of it against himself. But the repressed rage boils and steams and wants to emerge and does come to consciousness and gets deflected on his unsuspecting wife, his children and those people unfortunate enough to be his employees.

We remember Elvis Presley and Mama Cass and Freddie Prinze and Marilyn Monroe and Karen Carpenter and Edgar Rosenberg and Tennessee Williams and Truman Capote and Barbara Hutton and Howard Hughes and all the others. All of them were gifted people of considerable charm. All of them had money and fame and fortune and opportunity. All of them committed suicide in one form or another, the ultimate act of despair, hostility and self-destruction, because of emotional problems that were not addressed, understood or treated or well-treated.

In her recent autobiography, Gelsey Kirkland poignantly and painfully paints a life of great pain, of dissatisfaction, or incredible stress and self-hatred that led to anorexia, incessant and hopeless perfectionism, drug abuse, a series of disastrous relationships and hostility vented on the world. This breathtakingly beautiful woman, whose work was magical and a gift to the world, hated herself enough to make her life a horror. It struck me forcibly as I read the book that though Ms. Kirkland felt herself to have conquered these problems and be on a more positive road in life, and though I hope that is the case and I wish her that, how little I felt she understood the origin of her problems and how frightened I was that, if that were the case, she would be forced to continue to repeat them in one form or another.

In Kitty Kelly's unauthorized biography of Frank Sinatra, we experience a man who, though brilliantly gifted and graced by the gods of the world, and who, to all intents and purposes, is functioning better than most of us, nevertheless seems to be an ethical and moral monster and a psychologically seriously and morbidly disturbed personality who disgracefully used and abused thousands of people and who, himself, was so tortured that he, on several occasions, attempted suicide.

These anecdotes are snippets, not full realizations of the complex characterological strands and convolutions of personality and its functions, and do not, in any way, begin to elucidate the hundreds of thousands of ways that people operate in emotional illness to hurt themselves and others. They are merely random samplings, guideposts to my belief that in all charming, educated, functioning, well-suited elves there are goblins and gremlins, primed for trouble, capable of it and doing it, some in minor and many in major forms, and if we don't find ways to stop them in their tracks, they will move relentlessly toward mischief, mischief which has the self, the other, the society and the world at large for its playground.

That we hold on to the myth of denial about what mental health is and who we are is evidenced for me everywhere I look. We want to allocate "craziness" to a few on the fringe and ignore the pain and illness at our own core.

Several weeks ago I was having a conversation with an acquaintance, a doctor, about the general state of the world and to prove my point, illustrated it by several unnamed and unidentified episodes from the lives of my patients. His response was, "What do you expect from people who go to therapy?" I had many times told this man that all my people were intelligent and lovable, that most of them functioned as regular members of our society with jobs and friends and children, that some of them went beyond, into creative and cultural and societal contribution, indeed, that they were just like him. He could not admit that as he could not admit the greyness of his own life; that, in spite of his intelligence and hard work, he was stuck in a marriage that was not vital or satisfying; that he was burying his depression in his work and that he was smoking himself into an early grave. Several weeks after our conversation, a friend of mine who was a patient of this doctor called me with a story. Her 82 year old mother was living with her. This mother is an 82 year old woman who has had a minor stroke and has diabetes and a heart condition. There came a time when she was not able to swallow even liquids for 30 hours. Alarmed and disconcerted, my friend called this doctor, related the situation and asked him to see her mother. He dismissed the problems, sight unseen, as a reaction to the heat and joked that it would be good for this 82 year old woman to lose a couple of pounds. Fifteen minutes after the phone call, my friend's mother had a serious heart attack. This man's arrogance and lack of empathy and lack of responsibility had caused him to behave in such a way as to damage another—and to damage himself, because the incident eventually culminated in a malpractice suit. Yet he placed the problems in others, being totally unaware of the emotional problems inside himself that led him to hurt himself and others as well.

Several days ago, I had occasion to speak to a social worker who was the supervisor for an entire borough on child abuse issues. I had called her to complain about the very poor work executed by one of her workers in her dealings with one of my clients. We had a very pleasant conversation in which this seemingly competent, reasonable woman admitted that the proceedings had been non-productive and faulty and indeed abusive and that she would see to it that matters would be straightened out. Then she said, "The worker's first mistake was to place the children with your client. She should have checked, found out that the woman was in treatment, and then she would not have placed the children with her." I was aghast. That a trained social worker should have such prejudice and such ignorance was dumbfounding. The very fact that my client was in treatment was an indictment of her, sight unseen, rather than a testament to her strivings for health and well-being and for a more joyous life for herself. This worker would assume that some unknown foster home was more healthy for the children simply because the adults were not in treatment.

Sometimes the fear and the denial is so strong that it extends to total ignorance as to what psychotherapy is and the scope of its work. Recently, I was part of a theatrical production which included a fair number of people, all of them intelligent and gifted in their field. It was a revelation to me that many of these same people, generally knowledgeable and sophisticated and living in a metropolis like New York City, had little understanding of what it was I did and how and with whom I did it.

This individual denial and fear of knowing and doing is, of course, reflected in our government and society at large. We hear, in desultory contexts, statistics on drug abuse and homelessness and teenage suicide (one young person, under 24, commits suicide every 2 hours) and mass killings and adultery and divorce (50% divorce rate). However, nowhere is there an acknowledgement of all these issues under the umbrella of the mental health of our nation. Nowhere in our President's State of the Union Address are we alerted or enlightened to the State of the Union's emotional well-being. Nowhere does a senator or educator or congressman or mayor stand and offer a comprehensive mental health care plan for the people of our country. Nowhere is there a serious attempt for a task force or a dialogue or an investigation, at length and in great detail, about the mental and emotional well-being of our citizens, how that affects every strand of our lives, and how we are to move from where we are to where we ought to be.

Years ago, when President Carter made a serious attempt to address the issue, on some level, in a nationwide speech, mentioning the narcissism in our culture and some of the devastating effects it was having on our nation, he was misunderstood, ignored, misquoted and, two days later, forgotten.

Yet other countries, far less wealthy and powerful than we are, are able to address the reality and the central importance of the issue to their lives. In Denmark [*Woodmark Encyclopedia of the Nations: Europe*, Woodmark Press Ltd., John Wiley & Sons, New York, Toronto, Singapore 1976, p. 65], the state is primarily responsible for the care, education and support of both physically and mentally handicapped persons. Danish citizens may choose between two systems of primary health care: medical care provided free of charge by a doctor whom the individual chooses for a year and by those specialists, including psychologists and psychiatrists, to whom the doctor refers the patient; or complete freedom of choice of any doctor or specialist at any time with the state reimbursing two-thirds of the medical bills. In Sweden [p. 261], every citizen is guaranteed free medical and psychological care. Socialized health care, including psychological services, that is free is also present in Bulgaria, Czechoslovakia and Russia in its entirety. Great Britain [p. 310] has a comprehensive National Health Care Service, which provides full medical care to all residents of the United Kingdom. Included in this care are general medical care, dental care, pharmaceutical and optical services, hospital special services. Services are even available in patients' homes when necessary for both physical and mental illnesses. In Canada, patients are free, under the health insurance program, to choose their own general practitioners and specialists [*Statesman's Year Book*, John Paxton, St. Martin's Press, New York, 1987, p. 289].

In our society, people on Medicare have access to free mental health care. Yet, very often, they are unaware that it is a possibility for them. They are uneducated about the benefits of treatment and how to find it. People who so often are at a loss about how to manage their lives are doled out a monetary pittance, castigated, pitied, ignored, tolerated but not helped toward treatment which could be a road for them to self-esteem and better functioning. For our middle-class population, mental health care is an expensive, sometimes awesome proposition. There are psychiatrists in our system who charge $300.00 per session. The "normal" fee in New York City is $150.00 and a regular clinic fee where practitioners are often very young and inexperienced and transitory, is approximately $60.00. There are large numbers of people and families in our system who simply cannot afford the treatment they need and should receive.

In the days of the Renaissance, there was the concept of a Chain of Being, the idea that if something were malignant or corrupt or skewed in the Ruler, it would somehow, in time, work itself down on the populace at large, and inside the body politic as well as the individual life of its citizens. I suggest that the opposite is no less true. The untreated pain, suffering, problems, malignancy, skewed views and expectations, flaws of each of our individual peoples not only poison their lives but the common well of us all and results in the dismal living statistics that now exist in our country on how badly we are faring. A free mental health care preventative, diagnostic and treatment program for our country, together wth a massive educational program, liberally funded and dedicated to reach every stratum of our society as to a comprehensive understanding of mental health in all its manifestations, guises and possibilities, is essential to the healthy, loving functioning of the individuals, families and institutions of our country. Presently we measure success by money, fame and prosperity and we live in hell. Were we to measure success by the respect and love we accord ourselves and others, by our ability to cooperate, to solve problems, to educate well, to empathize with others, to share . . . we would live in heaven.

Another oft heard, well-known myth about therapy is that all you need to do is talk about your problems to friends and family, listen to advice and the issues will resolve themselves. "Why do I need a therapist? I have lots of people I can talk to." is a statement I often hear.

Having friends and family who can listen to you, hear you, empathize with you, who "are there for you," is a real blessing. Many of us don't have that kind of support system. We feel alone and lonely and alienated in our society and too often, as Lily Tomlin expresses it, "we are all in this alone." However, friends and family, though of great value, cannot substitute for or replace treatment. What we often mistake for the same thing are totally disparate processes. A good friend can know you, hug you, understand you, listen to you, give you advice. He cannot help you make your unconscious conscious; he cannot help you uncover the unknown rules and fantasies and phantoms and repetition compulsions by which you live; he cannot help you through an abandonment depression toward a more authentic self. For example, sexual abuse victims often have no memory of their abuse yet, unconsciously, have organized many of their life patterns around incidents they have no knowledge of. A friend cannot help one to retrieve the memories and associated feelings and to understand how present life patterns are a repetition of old trauma. When you have a temperature and nausea and a running bowel, a friend can provide the chicken soup and the cold compresses and he can hold your hand. He cannot diagnose or cure the illness.

Treatment does not take away from people their intelligence, their creativity or their individual talent. What it does is to help them understand themselves and the world better and to give them tools to mine the treasure which already exists.

Many people in our society, when they choose to go for help, will go indiscriminately, with the notion that every mental health professional is the same. Nothing could be further from the truth. We are not all the same. Another myth is that psychiatrists are better than psychologists and that psychologists are better than clinical social workers. Again, that has not been my experience. The quality of the treatment depends not on the particular degree, not on the fee charged, not on the celebrity of the practitioner and not even so much on the school of thought which the practitioner espouses, e.g., Freudian, Jungian, Sullivanian, behaviorist, etc., but most on the expertise and character of the specific, individual therapist. To choose a therapist is tricky business—there are as many charlatans in this field as in any other. So this choice must be approached with the same caution, carefulness, preparedness as the choice for a mate, for the repercussions can be as remarkable.

Firstly, it would be helpful for seekers to inform themselves about the specific treatment theories and modalities available. Someone who is religious and metaphysical might find himself more drawn to Jungian analysis than to Freud and might find himself with a Jungian therapist. It is not the purview of this book to explore the various psychotherapies—Jungian, Freudian, behaviorist, Kohut, self-psychology, interrelational, etc.—however, there are excellent books on the market to inform the prospective patient.

The second important step is not to indiscriminately pick a practitioner from the Yellow Pages and make an appointment and proceed. It is necessary to shop around, to interview two or three people, before settling on someone. It is important to feel comfortable with the person initially and to feel, from him or her, respect for you, your problems and your feelings. Perhaps the most advisable way to get the name of a therapist is to ask a person whom you respect, who is himself in therapy and is exhibiting good progress, or someone who is in the field and knows intensively the work of the person he recommends. I, myself, never refer to anyone whose work I don't personally know, even if he has a high visibility and reputation in the field, because how that person represents himself and his work may be at significant odds with the reality of how he practices. Once, when I was very young in the field, I referred a friend of mine who was having problems with her adolescent daughter to a man highly respected in adolescent psychiatry. At the time, this was a very depressed, overweight young lady who had cut off most of her own hair and was speaking to her parents only in swear words and who, of course, was deeply resistant to the idea of treatment. The psychiatrist promised that he would "charm" the young lady, that he was a charmer of young ladies—an odd statement, indeed—and proceeded to see the young lady for three sessions without ever helping her understand or even just telling her that treatment could help her with the pain and conflict she was experiencing. The mother was correctly aghast and the daughter used the non-statements as further resistance to the treatment she so badly needed. Doctors will often do what I did, refer to some colleague on the same staff or a family member or a practitioner with a "name" whose work they do not know.

The bottom line is that in so much of life, you are responsible for your own good treatment. You need to get recommendations from someone whose opinion you trust and who personally knows the quality of the work of the recommended practitioner. If that's not possible, then contact the mental health society in your area and ask for several names from them. Interview all these people (three or four) and settle not on the therapist who is being impressive or charming or seductive but on the one who is warm and respectful and who is really listening to who you are and what you have to say.

As the treatment goes on, one continues to need to be alert to the empathy the therapist pays to who you are, what you need and what your style is. The more the therapist is where you need to be at the moment, the more likely it is that he is an effective practitioner. Be very careful of a hidden agenda on the part of the therapist. This means that the therapist is pushing you in specific directions, not because that is what you want, not because that's where you are or need to be, but because of reasons and motivations of his own, either due to his lack of expertise in the process or due to his own personality problems. I will give a few examples to make it clear where the pitfalls lie. A colleague was coming to a point in her marriage where she was fully understanding and feeling the lack of respect her husband had always had for her needs, feelings, rights and entitlements. She felt enraged, disappointed, abused and convinced that she no longer wanted to spend her life with someone who was basically using her for his own ends. When she told her therapist that she was ready to divorce her spouse, he mumbled something about how her husband treated her better than she deserved. Astounded, because that was a total misconstruction of the facts, she confronted him on the statement. He would neither elaborate nor explore and concentrated instead on her "inappropriate" anger. She went home from the session bemused and confused and very hurt, only to discover that evening, from a colleague, that her therapist was in the midst of a very angry, messy divorce where the wife was accusing the husband of all manner of cruelty, including adultery. It became clear to my friend, then, that her therapist was not responding to her situation but rather to his own and was taking his feelings about his wife out on her. She attempted to work this counter-transference reaction out with the therapist but he wouldn't or couldn't. My friend left therapy with this man. Luckily, she had understood enough to know where the fault lay. Laypeople are in much more danger. Check the reality of the situation, the appropriateness of the therapist's response, raise questions if the relationship seems skewed in some confusing direction and don't hesitate to get a second opinion and check your feelings out with another, more objective person.

In another situation, a husband and wife went into couple counseling together with a female therapist. Within a couple of months of their beginning treatment the therapist suggested that they stop joint therapy and continue with her in individual treatment, each partner seeing her twice per week. Fairly soon after, in the individual sessions with the wife, the therapist began counseling her toward divorce proceedings. The couple were divorced, and the therapist subsequently married the husband.

In the midst of a midlife crisis that had precipitated a regression to infantile wishes, longing and rage, a man wanted to leave a marriage of twenty-five years. While friends and consulting therapists explained to him that he was in a state of depletion and regression and utter confusion and not fit to make any decision of that consequence, his own therapist fueled this rage and, instead of helping the patient understand its infantile origins in the primary family, colluded with him in foisting this rage on the present family to the point of the patient's leaving his home, cutting off support to the family and, in general, effecting disastrous results to himself and his family. Without intimate knowledge of the therapist, it is impossible to know whether this was a lack of competence, psychopathic behavior on the therapist's part or some counter-transferential collusion. Whatever the origin of the problem, the results were chaos and pain. The therapist continues to practice and is a respected staff member of a respected institute.

In another couple case, the wife was an extremely aggressive woman with no interest in the needs, wants or desires of her spouse. She had a very specific idea as to how she wanted to arrange her life. The husband, who was frightened of losing her and whose personality dynamic was to try as hard as possible to please the other so as to avoid punishment or abandonment, had nevertheless, through individual therapy, found some access to his own needs, feelings and wants, some of which were diametrically opposed to those of his wife. In couple counseling, for whatever conscious or unconscious reasons, the therapist quickly bought the wife's agenda and colluded with her in manipulating and menacing the man into places and positions in which he didn't want to be. It was only with careful and consistent work in his individual sessions that the man was able to understand what was occurring in the couple counseling and to extricate himself from a very unfortunate situation.

Recently, in a much milder case, a woman, a therapist herself, became infatuated with a man in whom she saw very unique, admirable and special qualities. However, being very knowledgeable, observant and astute herself, she could not help but notice that this very same man for whom she felt a deep attraction was also remote, passive, dismissive of people and angry when crossed or challenged in any way. Perturbed and disturbed, she brought this into her treatment and pondered letting go this fledgling possibility, because to her the difficulty of a relationship with such a man was already clear. Again, for unknown reasons of her own, the therapist became the man's advocate, acknowledging that there were some problems but coating them in general chocolate icing, explaining that men were different from women and finding rationalizations for his acting-out. Fueled by her own attraction to this man and her own therapist's agenda in giving the go-ahead, the woman began the relationship, only to find that, of course, she had been right all along and if she had followed her own intuition, knowledge and reason, she would have saved herself pain, time and energy.

These examples are not prohibitive but cautionary. There are wonderful workers out there who will help you find the life you want for yourself. But there are also others who are steering you not in your own direction but in theirs, and that's one of the central issues on which every one of us patients must keep a vigilant eye.

You have now been with a therapist for six months. You feel comfortable with the person; you trust that he cares about you, that he listens to you, that he is respectful of who you are and what your goals are in life and in treatment. Good. However, by six months something should have begun to happen. You might have access to feelings you never had before; you might have some insight into yourself or some understanding of people or the world that is new to you; you might have suddenly developed some psychosomatic symptoms; you might be dreaming and remembering your dreams for the first time in your life. You should be beginning the process. If, between six months and a year, nothing seems to be happening, you're going, you're paying and you're feeling only frustration and boredom and a sense of failure, stop and examine very carefully what is going on. Talk seriously about it to your own therapist and think seriously about consulting someone else to evaluate the work.

Therapy is a serious process, often long and hard and unique to each patient and each partnership. As a patient, you will feel exhaustion and surprise and a sense of delight and boredom and failure and hope and anxiety. You will love your therapist at times and you will hate your therapist at times. Sometimes you will run to sessions and find the time evaporating before you know it. Sometimes you will hate the thought of coming, and sometimes you will purposefully not come. Throughout the stops and gos and highs and lows of this adventure, never be afraid to ask your therapist questions or to share with him—indeed—absolutely share with him what you are thinking, feeling and experiencing. He should treat this very carefully, reverentially, respectfully and thoroughly. If he doesn't, he's not a therapist for you. And, throughout this exhilarating and difficult adventure, keep your eye on the main issue. Am I getting better? Is my life getting better? Are my relationships more honest, more harmonious, more fulfilling? Do I know more about myself, more about other people, more about the world, about how to solve problems, more about what my own past was really about and how it's affecting my present? Be advised that, throughout this process, there will operate in you unconscious, masochistic persuasive mechanisms, urging you to leave treatment and fighting to hang on to the old order. If you have a good therapist and the process is helping, fight to hang in there and proceed; though you may not find yourself in a rose garden, you will eventually find yourself in a much sunnier, healthier, more loving, more productive place for you and those whose lives you touch.

A very recent myth about therapy is what's called "brief psychotherapy." The proposition is that in ten to twelve sessions, a very seasoned and expert psychotherapist can help a patient gain relief from his symptoms and pain and deadness, from his non-productive life patterns, and return him to a more fulfilling, productive, happier life. Indeed, in the last year or so, there have emerged people who say they can accomplish this in one session and are offering themselves as both practitioners and trainers of other practitioners.

This is a very appealing concept on numerous levels. For the patient, it suggests that he can "get better" very quickly and without great cost to himself in either money, time, energy, pain, uncertainty . . . who would not want that, especially in our instant gratification, "feel good" society? For the practitioner it suggests an endless stream of patients (who would not come if they could get better in ten sessions?) and, therefore, an endless stream of money. It is also very helpful to practitioners who are inept and at a loss. It's much easier to muddle through and fake your way through ten sessions rather than five years of sessions. For practitioners who are afraid of intimacy or the dependence of the patient or the murderous rage of the patient, very little of this will emerge in the twelve sessions. For practitioners who can't do or can't stand the ongoing vigorous search, journey, the times of bewilderment and not knowing of what's happening, the patient's ongoing, endless laments and depression, the quest for meaning in complex dreams and amorphous metaphors and images, short-term therapy will relieve them of all that. For the insurance companies, this is surely a boon. How much better to be liked for $600 rather than for $2,000? How much more money and profit for the companies! The needs of all the partners are being met and satisfied. But are they?

To me, this is yet another hoax, another codependent relationship where people are blinding themselves to the truth and aligning to exist in lies and destructiveness. When a person comes to treatment, he comes with a set of symptoms and character formations that have had years to rigidify and coalesce. Like a computer, the patient is vigorously programmed to be on automatic, to exhibit and maintain the consistent program forever. Each of a patient's actions is multi-determined; that means they are caused by numerous incidents and feelings, serve different conflict patterns, involve different organs and are programmed to repeat compulsively. For example, a person will enter treatment with a specific symptom—say, migraine headaches. This one symptom is composed of a variety of strands, e.g., a rigid superego that demands perfection, the person's need to punish himself when he makes mistakes or doesn't achieve perfection, the use of that symptom to allow oneself to be passive so that one can escape from the daily demands for perfectionistic acting, a specific choice of the head because the person was often told that he was "stupid" and "stupidity" resides in the head, a repetition of this particular symptom when it was modeled by a parent . . . etc. It will take much time and effort to uncover the strands and origins of this one symptom and much more time to help the patient understand the dynamics and to help him lighten the rigid superego, allow himself passivity and leisure without resorting to headaches. How can this be done in twelve sessions? And this is *one* symptom. We are speaking of many symptoms and patterns. It can't. And those who tell you it can are incompetent, not knowledgeable, unethical or immoral.

Once in a while, we have a very particular problem that arises in our lives. A child is going through adolescence. A child who has been formerly loving and appropriate and well-functioning suddenly becomes angry, rebellious, passive; grades slip, grandiosity flourishes. A first-time parent may be bewildered by this shift, ignorant of what it means, anxious about possible horrendous outcomes and at a loss for strategies since old parent strategies are not working in this new phase. This may be a time to see a professional and explore the situation. It is possible that if both parent and child are fairly healthy emotionally, eight, ten, twelve sessions will be enough to understand the facts and the feelings and to give information, support and age-appropriate parental techniques. In another situation, a man came because though he loved his wife very much, they enjoyed each other and were both satisfied with their life, child and lifestyle, he had stopped feeling great, passionate sexual attraction to his wife and it concerned him. He wondered what that meant, what to do and how to handle his sexual feelings and fantasies about other women and their attendant guilt feelings. In a third situation, a woman came into treatment because after a twenty-five year marriage and a three year period of mourning, she suddenly found herself on the dating scene. Bewildered by what she experienced as a totally "new world"—unfamiliar rules, games and expectations—she sought some help to orient herself emotionally and practically in a new and strange situation that seemed to have nothing in common with her previous dating experience. These are all situational issues, phase of life problems where we ourselves are changing or where our situation has altered in a relationship or in the world—a spouse has died; a divorce has occurred; a child is moving on; we suddenly become aware of the aging process; we've lost a cherished job and we're faced with difficult facts and feelings that are hard to handle or understand. Again, if one is a well-organized personality, emotionally healthy and strong, through either constitutional make-up, good parenting or previous good intensive long-term psychotherapy or all three, brief psychotherapy may be a helpful and productive option.

Unfortunately, however, there are few strong, well put together, emotionally healthy people in our midst and very few relatively simple life situations. For the most part, people are troubled, tenuously put together, functioning on automatic and seriously ignorant of who they really are and what reality is really about, and most life situations are complex, multi-determined, complicated, long-term and painful. To "fix" the majority of people and their issue is a serious long-term task where both the patient and the therapist need to have the tenacity, diligence and patience to do the "hard work" over a period of years. A new patient of mine recently came for treatment to me because she found herself in her middle years, with both her children gone and married, without a life. She found herself deeply depressed, unable to pursue her talent and alone, having withdrawn from family and friend relationships. It emerged that she had had another experience in treatment with a therapist that she had seen for about a year who had helped to lift her depression and strategize her relationships with family members and then pronounced her "cured." This former therapy had not addressed her very negative self-image and its origins, her dreams with their associations to possible incest, the specificities of her guilt-laden queen-slave relationship with her mother and her wounding relationship with a sibling . . . since these and other very serious issues were not addressed, understood or worked through, they remained in her psyche, quietly acting-out and producing distressing and destructive symptoms and patterns until, with the leaving of her last child, they seized the opportunity of separation grief, to emerge full-blown and in full force.

In most cases, brief psychotherapy is akin to placing a Band-Aid over a festering, blistering wound. The wound may feel better for a while, may be more hidden and less apparent, but it will continue to hurt and to fester and to be refilled with blistering poison because it has not been cleaned or healed at its source and not adequately treated.

One of the chief proponents of brief psychotherapy is a senior practitioner, very much respected in his field. At a recent seminar given by him, when asked why he was encouraging brief psychotherapy as a major option for people and how this treatment modality had emerged for him as viable, he stated that he began doing it while working at the V.A. hospital because the hospital would not allow more than a series of sessions for treatment, and he continued to do it and was "marketing" it because he felt that presently and in the future both people and insurance companies would not be amenable to long-term "depth" psychotherapy. Frankly, this statement was astounding to me and struck me as extremely "Madison Avenue." "Find out what the people want and give it to them," whether it be healthy, helpful, productive or not! Simultaneously, it reminded me of a bad mother who wanted to be popular with her kids and therefore could set no limits but allowed them to eat French fries, hotdogs and ice cream unconscious so that we can meet our demons, slay them, transform them and emerge into the sunlight of a happier, healthier life.

Rabbi Aryeh Levine is considered by many Jewish scholars to be one of the great Jewish saints of this century [*A Tzaddik in Our Time*,

Simcha Raz]. Once when Reb Aryeh's wife suffered pain in her feet, he went with her to the doctor and told him, "My wife's feet are hurting us." Thus, one person's pain is all our pain. We must join together—patients, doctors, government, society—to alleviate it.

LEGENDS

Sometimes the lies we feed ourselves and each other, the illusions of how we would like things to be, the infantile idealization we crave, the self-wishes that seem impossible for us cohere into stories that we create and tell each other about other people. Someone becomes a "perfect" human being, the archetype of goodness, genius, sexuality, feminism . . . These beings have no flaws, no sins, no "dark and grained spots." They walk on water and move through life in clouds of joy. We create legends. We create myths. We create lies.

In 1932, Stark Young, a leading drama critic of his day [*Garbo*, Antoni Gronowicz, Simon and Schuster, 1990, p. 451] wrote the following about Greta Garbo: "She presents an instance of the natural and right progress of the poetic from the concrete toward ideality." He continues to use phrases like "the remote entity of her spirit," "a certain noble poignancy in her presence." Thus we see a piece of the Garbo legend—Ms. Garbo as noble, poetic, elevated . . . Indeed, Ms. Garbo was none of those things. From a poor and highly dysfunctional family, she stole merchandise from the department store she worked in, permitted herself to be "created" into a false image by Maurice Stiller, who stole money for an opportunity to begin his career, permitted herself to be sold to the Hollywood establishment and the moviegoing public in none of her truth and all of her fabrication and dedicated her life to making money and preserving her legend. When her creator and benefactor was ousted from Hollywood and had to return to Europe, desperate and penniless, she did not accompany him as they had promised each other and did nothing to help him or support him or reward him for creating her, establishing her and "selling" her legend. For years, she had a liaison with George Schlee, who was a long-married man and whose wife Valentine had long been Garbo's supposed friend. One night when she sees him very pale and inert, "falling down on his bed," she leaves the room, goes peacefully to sleep in her own room, without any worries or concerns, and finds him dead the next morning [p. 420]. Seeing him dead, she leaves the hotel and Paris without even notifying the hotel authorities. She then decides not to see her "friend" Valentine anymore, to move out of the apartment where they were neighbors and to avoid their mutual friends. Having immersed herself in a marriage of long duration, she proceeded to confess that "perhaps our love was more on George's side than mine. Naturally I liked it that someone was devoted to making me happy and doing anything possible to help me. Later, that someone got tired and went away or I got tired and disappeared. Then, somebody else would come and take his place. Or die." She espoused no causes, gave nothing to charity, created no foundations but spent her life only on herself—hardly the life of a noble and poetic soul.

Kenneth Tynan is representative of the critics and the public who immortalized Garbo as the most feminine, sexual, sensual woman on earth, the irresistible woman with whom all men fall in love and who represents boundless sexual allure. "'What when drunk, one sees in other women, one sees in Garbo sober" [Tynan, p. 452]. Roland Barthes [p. 452] wrote, "She is a sort of platonic ideal of the human creature . . . descended from heaven where all things are formed and perfected in the clearest light" . . . In fact, Ms. Garbo was bisexual, with clearly masculine traits (gait, voice, etc.). She reports, herself, the wisdom of a conversation with Countess Wachtmeister where the countess says, "You are not a full woman and you are not a full man. Everything depends on the season of your soul. One day, you are a woman, and the next day, you are a man. . ." [p. 355]. Indeed, Ms. Garbo's disenchantment and disappointment in heterosexual sex is clearly stated, "I discovered that the mutual caressing and delicate handling of two people of the same sex was more soothing than the activities that took place between the two different sexes. I even found that masturbation is more rewarding than sexual intercourse between male and female" [p. 309]. Is it not ironic that this bisexual woman who never really valued passionate sex, who was incapable of love, who was truly narcissistic ("Next to fame, the second most important thing is money. I love it" [p. 316]) should be relegated to the personification of feminine beauty, romance, love and sexuality and nobility?

It is fascinating to read in Garbo's biography by Antoni Gronowicz how well she understood and perpetuated the lies of her legend. She knew that the persona created for her by Maurice Stiller of an elegant, remote, unreachable and unattainable woman who "wants to be alone" was a minute, total fabrication from the underwear he selected to the clever ploy he devised for her to shun publicity while other stars were chasing it. And she knew that later stories "leaked" to the press were equal lies.

> The press stories, which, I suspected,
> were leaked by Galord Hauser, Cecil
> Beyton, Fleur Cowles, John Gunther, Clare
> Booth Luce, Baron Erich Goldschmidt
> Rothchild, and a hundred others, amazed
> and amused me very much." [. 411]

> Although I didn't know any of these
> people very well, by which I mean that I
> didn't have a special affection for them
> or any kind of special relationship with
> them, it seemed they knew every thought
> of mine, past, present and future. There
> was talk of my "inexhaustible spiritual
> assets" and, of course, of my physical
> beauty. I was compared to practically
> everyone in history, including St.
> Francis of Assisi and Salome. These
> people became the propagators of my
> legend, although they also disoriented
> the public by spreading untrue stories.
> But I knew that my legend grew each time
> my name was mentioned on the radio or in
> the press. Surprisingly enough, the
> general public believed these stories
> because the people who originated them
> were highly placed in the worlds of
> literature, arts and finance.

> I did not confirm or deny the rumors
> about me. Instead, I would return to my
> room, lock my door, and laugh until my
> stomach hurt. I could not imagine how a
> simple woman like me was able to occupy
> the minds of outstanding writers, artists
> and millionaires. If somebody engaged me

in serious conversation about social,
cultural or political affairs, I did not
know how to respond. Any man or woman
who induced me to have sexual relations
became disenchanted because my impulses
were false and my reactions to physical
stimuli were superficial. People who
told exciting stories about me didn't
know me and actually were hoping to have
closer contact. I knew what they wanted
so I deliberately postponed close
relations, hoping that the hide and seek
would go on longer and I would profit by
the publicity. It was a game between a
cast of powerful and clever cats and a
little mouse, me. My legend was the
nourishment of my life; I had no deeper
interest. Even war and peace did not
interest me much, although I once
ventured to say in a social gathering
that the Soviet soldiers who were beating
back Hitler's army were outrageous and
beautiful. This story reaches the press
and I received praise and invitations
from Communist groups all over the world.
So even Communists created publicity for
a confused woman. Somehow people had a
total belief in me and were willing to
sacrifice their reputations and time to
publicize me.

And we, the "little, average" people, are more than willing to swallow the lies, aid and abet their influence and perpetuate them unto eternity.

John Lennon was the creator and star of The Beatles, the "hottest" singing group in the extravagant sixties. This was a group that was revered by zillions for their music and who made zillions in making the music. John, himself, aside from being a pop idol and expounded as the greatest guitarist of the Rock Age, was celebrated in life as a guru of peace, love and understanding and, when he died, was mourned, in death, as the martyred saint of the international peace movement. During his marriage to Yoko Ono, they represented themselves as the perfect couple, one in their love, one in their art, one in their efforts for international peace. John portrayed himself as coming from a poverty background and difficult circumstances and designated himself as a working-class hero.

Nothing of the representation, noting of the legend was truth. John's family was not ruinously poor when he was born. The family's home was located in a desirable district in Liverpool and was provided with both an indoor toilet and a backyard. The boy was well provided for and sent to Infants' school. When he was given into the care of his aunt Mimi, he lived in Mendips, a seven room semi-detached house in a middle-class suburb. He was forbidden by his aunt to play with any children save those chosen by Mimi, all children of the upper class. John had a treehouse and a back garden and was encouraged in reading, writing and painting. Television and comic books were not permitted [*The Lives of John Lennon*, Albert Goldman, William Morrow & Co., 1988, p. 40]. Instead, John read the *Just William* books, the comic misadventures of an upper middle-class boy in an affluent nowhere land. He was taught to say mater and pater, he was sent to a classy British high school, and his studies were designed to fit him for a professional life. Every summer until he was fifteen, he was sent off to his aunt's town house and, then, onto the family sheep farm on the northernmost coast of Scotland.

As to his musical genius, John Lennon, when a child, was given an accordion upon which he learned to play the hits of the day. Next he learned to play the harmonica, and then, after hearing Elvis' "Heartbreak Hotel," he convinced his mother to buy a battered old Spanish guitar and she taught him to play it as if it were a banjo, tuning the top five strings to G and allowing the bottom strings to flop. At that time, thousands of British boys banded together in skiffle bands, John Lennon among them. Thus John Lennon had no formal musical training of any kind, no rigorous instruction of musical theory or practice, no hours of practicing, just a capacity for tinkering, chutzpah and adoration of Elvis, Little Richard and rock and roll.

Not everyone was taken in by The Beatles and their musical genius legend. Muhammed Ali said of Ringo Starr that his dog plays better drums [p. 91]; David Spinoza, one of the consummate musicians of that era, had this to say about Paul McCartney: "He played those basic rock 'n' roll things—ching, ching, ching. It was embarrassing! He had to sing every note or hit it on his guitar, like the three notes of the major seventh. He didn't even know what the chord was called. He called it the 'pretty chord.'" Paul himself confessed that The Beatles were criminals, plagering material from other people's music, and John disclosed [p. 137] that the hook used in both "I Feel Fine" and "Day Tripper" was filched from an unsuspected source. Both John Lennon and George Harrison were formally charged in court with plagiarism and had to make restitution. Reviews of *The Ed Sullivan Show* [1964] found The Beatles highly disappointing. The *Herald Tribune* labeled them as 5% publicity, 20% haircut and 5% lilting element. *The New York Times* saw the group as a "fine mass placebo." *News eek* proclaimed: "Visually, they are a nightmare; tight, dandified, Edwardian beatnick suits and great pudding bowls of hair. Musically, they are a near disaster, guitars and drums slamming out a merciless beat that does away ith secondary rhythms, harmony and melody. Their lyrics are a catastrophe, a preposterous farrago of Valentine-card romantic sentiments." In spite of all this, in spite of George Martin shaking his head on The Beatles' musical illiteracy on the set of "The Making of *Sergeant Pepper*," their continued drug-taking, their inability to communicate because each described different ideas in vague non technical language, their *Ed Sullivan Show* appearance drew 73,900,000 viewers, the largest audience in the history of television. *Sergeant Pepper* was a "shout heard around the world" and John and The Beatles made zillions of dollars and became worldwide celebrities and legends.

As for John and Yoko embodying the essence of romance, love, marriage and parenting, those were yet another barrage of lies and publicity stunts engineered by the Lennons to enhance their celebrity. In truth, the Lennons, living in the Dakota, seldom saw each other. John spent his day in the bedroom, feasting on a macrobiotic diet and drugs that reduced him to anorexia and mindlessness. Once or twice a day, for half an hour at a time, he might emerge to the kitchen, to throw rages, sometimes kicking Sean and once pitching a cat down the hall. In his trance, he was often plagued by colds and fever, indigestion, dizzy spells. At one point, he was so deeply depressed that he didn't leave his room for six months. As for Yoko, "she mainly ignores him, saying she's very busy" [p. 18]. When he wants to speak to her on the phone, he has to make an appointment with a member of her staff. He is not allowed to enter her office when she is on the phone, as she is day and night, wheeling and dealing, since she has full responsibility of the business, having been given power of attorney by John who made her his proxy in every business matter. Yoko handled matters so well that, at the end, she was in such financial trouble that six accountants couldn't come up with any solution except that she borrow money from whatever bank at whatever interest.

As for the romantic coupling of John and Yoko: Before John met Yoko, she had already slept with any man who could possibly do her any good. Married to her second husband before she was divorced from the first, she was capable of much violence towards others and toward herself such as keeping her husband prisoner in the bathtub with a shard of glass, threatening him with butcher knives and, on more than one occasion, trying to kill herself. Her meeting with John was far from accidental. She was chasing him, finding ways to run into him, although she knew full well that he was married. She planted a ring at his mother-in-law's so that she would have an excuse to return and sent John notes, threatening that she would commit suicide if he didn't send her money to support her art. According to the Lennons' "Hollywood fantasy," eighteen months elapsed between the lovers' meeting and consummation of their passion. In reality, the time between meeting and mating was exactly three weeks. All this time Yoko was feeding John lies that she was the creator of flower power, the founder of The Happening. . .

During the years of the marriage, the Lennons often existed in a stupor of heroin, cocaine, hashish, LSD, marijuana and amphetamine pills. Yoko surrounded herself with psychics and exerted incredible influence by alleging that everything she wanted people to do was directed by the psychics and the stars. Once she ordered John to fly home in a westerly direction from Japan, which meant a twenty-five hour journey. He was appalled but he did it. When she didn't want to be bothered having sex with John, she talked May Pang into being his mistress. When she wanted John back, she got him back, using magic and psychics and "hypnosis": in a way John himself could not comprehend. When John, at one point, finally felt strong enough to contemplate an album and made plans, she yelled, harangued and terrified him into a joint album. Power-hungry, she controlled John and controlled the media. At one point, she ordered a skywriting event to celebrate Sean and John's birthday to establish herself as a good wife and mother when all the while she was planning to divorce John and was carrying on a torrid affair with Sam Green to the very end. Yoko, the consummate narcissist, cared nothing for John, his wishes, his feelings or his needs, listening only to her own self-centered dictates. She had John cremated—John, who had a horror of cremation and had specifically asked for and wanted funeral rites.

In their parenting, John and Yoko repeated the neglect and abandonment and abuse that they had suffered as children. With Julian, John was either physically absent, due to weeks and months on the road, or, when he was home, emotionally absent because he created a cocoon for himself, a room in the house where he sunned, slept, watched television and paid attention to no one. When Julian did appear [p. 193], John would growl and yell Julian into terrified silence, and then tap his head and indicate that there was something "wrong" with the boy, "a bit of a dope, like mother, like son." After he divorced Cynthia, John saw Julian only rarely. Yoko repeated the same pattern with her child. After she divorced Tony Cox, she did not see her child, Kyoko Cox, virtually abandoning her, until years later when she and John decided to kidnap the unfortunate girl when she was seven and living with her father in Majorca. The child was only seven, desperately terrified and agitated when she realized what was happening, and, when the Lennons were apprehended, begged the judge to see her daddy. Yoko lost her first Lennon baby in a miscarriage [p. 319], probably triggered by a beating that she received from John and by an arrest for possession of a variety of drugs. Yoko had Sean, their second child, removed by Cesarean section on John's birthday, one month before he was due. Yoko admitted that this was purposefully done due to psychic advice. Tended by a nanny (not his mother), Sean, at four, was not yet weaned or toilet trained. "He is permitted to do anything he wants, smearing the white walls with paint or urinating all over the backseat of the limousine. When Sean is not being cared for by his nanny, he is being cared for by Marnie (Marlene) Hair, the Lennon neighbor and confidant. It is she who watches during the day over the playing of the children, and it is at her house that he shares a bed every night with her son Caitlin."

What can we say about John Lennon as a man of gentleness and peace, as an advocate of peace and as an altruist who sought to cure

103

the ills of the world? John Lennon was such an angry child that at five and a half he was expelled from kindergarten for hitting and beating up on other children. When he was an adolescent [p. 48], he blew up street lamps with homemade bombs, stuffed firecrackers into letter boxes, filched records from shops, pulled down girls' pants in public and would generally attempt to discover people's secrets and humiliate them in public. He rolled soldiers, taking their money, and thought he had killed one. Later, as a "star," he got very drunk and ruined the Smothers Brothers' opening by shouting obscenities and singing at the top of his voice. At a club atop The Rainbow Room, a group of fans were shouting at him from the parking lot. Incensed, he ran outside and started punching those fans nearest him. When he was with May, he tried to kill her in the Jacuzzi, throwing her into a wall and beating her up as he had beaten up Yoko. He is reputed to almost have killed Bob Wooler [p. 141], a disc jockey, because he thought that Bob knew about his affair with Brian Epstein. The Lennons were infatuated with criminally inclined demagogues [p. 377] such as Michael X, a one-time pimp whom the British government deported to his native Trinidad, where he was tried and convicted for double murder. When warned that if The Beatles bought a Greek island as a retreat, they would be playing right into the hands of the Fascist regime, John expounded, "I don't care if the government is all Fascist or communists . . . They're all the same." When Yoko and John were doing their bed-ins for peace and when they were chanting "give peace a chance," they were deeply strung out on dope. When they preached peace, they were also supporting violence. They supported the I.R.A. and financed riots in Miami. When the political convention commenced in the summer of 1972, A.J. Webberman (a leading member of the Rock Liberation Front) took two busloads of Zippas across the state lines to disrupt the proceedings, and John paid for this.

Some sayings attributed to John Lennon, a man of the people, for the people:

> On Martin Luther King's assassination:
> "Who the hell cares who murdered the nigger?"

> From John's Japan diary: "Basically, I
> don't like people."

About women: "Women should be obscene and
not heard."

About friendship: "I don't have any
friends. Friendship is a romantic illusion."

About his fans: "They are an ugly race
and their ancestors, the hippies, are
uptight maniacs going around wearing
fucking peace symbols. I resent
performing for 'fucking idiots."

About an associate: "Creepy Jewboy—they
should have stuck you in the oven with
the rest of them."

In 1980, Laurence Shames wrote an article for *Esquire* entitled
"John Lennon, Where Are You? In Search of the Beatle Who Spent
Two Decades Seeking True Love and Cranial Bliss Only to Discover
Cows, Daytime Television and Palm Beach Real Estate." Basically,
the article exposed Lennon, whom millions views as the "conscience
of his generation," as "a typical seventies type—a forty year old
businessman who's got $150 million . . . good lawyers to squeeze him
through tax loops . . . who's stopped making errors and stopped
making music."

Fred Seaman was John's companion for a time, towards the end of
John's life. What shocked and bewildered Seaman [p. 637] was
"simply the eccentricity of the Lennon household and the total
disparity between the Lennons' real life and the image they presented
to the world."

Harold Seider, a lawyer, advisor and counselor to the Lennons in
matters of business, says this about the Lennons, "The real Lennon
was not the public statements he made. He didn't give a shit about
lying because, to a certain extent, he had contempt for the media
because they bought all that crap; he was there to manipulate the
media. He enjoyed doing that. He understood how to use the media. . .
it was not that they believed it but that was the image they wanted to
present."

Simone de Beauvoir is known and respected all over the world for being one of the generals and innovators in the fight for feminism. Her book *The Second Sex* is and has been, for approximately fifty years, touted as a call to arms for women's equality and a staple in the canon of women's studies. In it, she describes the woeful plight of women regulated to a secondary, submissive position in the world.

> History has shown us that men have always
> kept in their hands all concrete powers;
> since the earliest days of the
> patriarchete, they have thought it best
> to keep women in a state of dependence;
> their code of laws have been set up
> against her, and thus she has definitely
> been established as the other. [*The
> Second Sex*, p. 134]

> Now, woman has always been man's
> dependent, if not his slave, the two
> sexes have never shared the world in
> equality. [p. xxiv]

> What peculiarly signals the situation of
> woman is that—a free and autonomous
> being, like all human creatures,
> nevertheless finds herself living in a
> world where men compel her to assume the
> status of others. [. xxxv]

> The husband "forms" his wife—not
> erotically alone but also morally and
> intellectually, he educates her, marks
> her, sets his imprint upon her . . . And
> woman is par excellence, the "clay" in
> his hands which can be passively shaped
> and worked. [p. 179]

> Furthermore, like all the oppressed,
> woman deliberately dissembles her

objective actuality; the slave, the
servant, the indigent, all who depend
upon the caprices of a master, have
learned to turn toward him a changeless
smile or an enigmatic impassivity; their
real sentiments, their actual behavior
are carefully hidden. [p 259]

He projects upon her what he desires and
what he fears, what he loves and what he
hates. And, if it is difficult to say
anything specific about her, that is
because man seeks the whole of himself in
her and because she is all . . . Being
all, she is never quite this which she
should be; she is everlasting deception,
the very deception of that existence
which is never successfully attained or
fully reconciled with the totality of
existants. [p. 197]

De Beauvoir perceived women as leading lives of secondary beings, without status or power or equality or choice, without dignity or respect, needing to use all their "wiles" to find and keep a protector in this world, and then submitting themselves to him for use and abuse. "All male ideologies are directed at justifying the oppression of woman . . . women are so conditioned by society that they consent to this oppression" [*All Said and Done*, 1971, p. 544].

What Simone de Beauvoir advocated for women was equality, no "domestic drudgery," no submissive-dominating relationships, full independence, strict concentration on her own work, career, art, no putting herself aside for another, her needs for another's needs, full cooperation, reciprocity, honesty, fidelity in relationships between men and women. What she advocated for others, she claimed to have achieved herself, in her life and in her relationship with Jean-Paul Sartre.

I don't think there was anything special
about myself in regard to those other

women except that I had more willpower
and a much sharper understanding of
myself than they did. No man has ever
asked me to fetch his coffee or iron his
clothes, because I have no intention of
doing it for anyone, myself or others and
they probably sensed that. I believed
that if women felt about themselves as I
felt about myself there would be none of
this caretaking that led to so many
misunderstandings by men of the role of
women. I've often said this and it bears
repeating, that *because I have never felt
discrimination among men in my life*, I
refused to believe that it existed for
other women . . . [*Biography of Simone de
Beauvoir*, Deidre Bair, p. 339]

We had a relationship based on total
equality, reciprocity, a complete
relationship. For one thing, I admired
Sartre a good deal and I still do. But
this does not mean I consider myself
second-rate or that he considered me that
way either . . . [p. 174]

I am fortunate to enjoy a *perfect*
relationship with both a man and a woman.
[p. 512]

Persistently and consciously, Simone de Beauvoir presented herself to the world as the authentic role model for the "equal" woman and her relationship with Sartre as the embodiment of how a man and woman should be together. There is no doubt that she succeeded in getting much of the world to believe her. There is equally no doubt that what she presented and fought so hard all her life to maintain was a myth and bears little resemblance to the actual facts of her life.

At the very beginning of their relationship, after they had become lovers, Georges, Simone's father, accosted Sartre and demanded that there be a marriage. Vague and flustered, Sartre "hinted" at marriage and they spoke about it, deciding against it. It seems very strange that a young women from her conventional background should refuse the proposal of a man she so adored that she was willing to risk her family's ostracism to be with him. Since they avowed how much they wanted to spend all their waking moments together, marriage would seem the obvious answer. What most likely happened is that the perpetually adolescent Sartre "hinted" at marriage in such a fashion as to make it clear that he would have none of it, and de Beauvoir, who almost always "fell into line," acquiesced. That it was not what she really wanted is substantiated by a quote of hers made toward the end of her life [*Biography*, p. 156] when she explained patiently, hit with residual bitterness, "Marriage was impossible. I had no dowry."

In the early period of their life together, Sartre and de Beauvoir were separated since Sartre was at his military station in Tours and de Beauvoir was in Paris at the Lycée Duruy. They spent some weekends together. "The weekends that they were not together and the days between weekends were long and lonely, and the emptiness of her life overwhelmed her. She had invested everything in him and when he wasn't with her, she felt herself less than nothing" [p. 165].

She read the lists of books he sent her, guiding her intellectual life. She tried to model herself after him, seeing him as her mentor and role model. He told her she must become a writer and so she tried that. He expected her to adopt every aspect of his thinking and she did. All this is hardly the action of an independent, "equal" woman, living in an independent, equal relationship. That the relationship was not one of reciprocity, cooperation, compromise and respect between two adults of equal power was evident from the very beginning. During his military tour, Sartre applied for an appointment in Japan-an annual lectureship sponsored by the French government. He was undeterred by the fact that he would have to leave de Beauvoir behind. Terrified, she began to hunt for schemes to accompany him, or at least not to be left behind in Paris, even thinking briefly of going to Budapest to teach French and English, although she spoke English with an appalling accent. When Sartre was refused the Japan appointment, he took a post teaching philosophy in Le Havre with no concern that this would again separate him from his lover. His lover, desperate to be with him, asked her father to help her find a job in Paris . . . any job . . . as long as it would allow her weekends with Sartre. Again, this obviously is the action of a clinging woman who has put herself and her interests and her career and her authentic future aside to be able to "follow her man." These are not the actions of a woman committed to her own self and her own special destiny or the events of a relationship between equals.

As it began, so it continued. She did not discuss books with him that she read but that she knew he would not be interested in. She put her own reading aside immediately and without question when he wanted her literary assistance. Even, in later years, when she was constantly writing and publishing and needing to adhere to deadlines, she would include as part of her daily work reading and commenting upon his and putting hers immediately aside whenever he needed her. She could ask for his help, only sometimes, only when something deeply troubled her, only after he had finished his stint of writing and only at his convenience. Her secondary role in the relationship, her wish not to know it, her inability not to know it and her ambivalence about it are all expressed in this quote:

> His work was more important than mine.
> I discovered that he was far more
> creative than I. Naturally, I bowed to
> this and put it before my own. I would
> have been very silly not to.
> We had a relationship based on total
> equality, reciprocity, a complete
> relationship. For one thing, I admired
> Sartre a good deal and I still do. But
> this does not mean consider myself
> second-rate or that he considered me that
> way wither. So why do I concern myself
> with his work before mine? I could
> indeed have busied myself with my own,
> but if he came before mine, so be it.
> [*Biography*, p. 174]

The pattern of their relationship which continued throughout their lives was one defined mainly by his needs and choices. When, after

Le Havre, Sartre took a position in Berlin, de Beauvoir allowed it although she had been totally miserable when separated from him: "He wanted to go to Berlin so badly that naturally, I wanted it for him as well" [p. 188]. She wanted their money to be kept independent, he wanted it shared, so they shared it. She did not ask him whether he had told his father about her because she felt he wouldn't like it. She did not like or trust Olga, one of Sartre's mistresses, but would not even allow herself her own feelings and thoughts: "Little by little, however, I began to compromise: my need to agree with Sartre on all subjects outweighed the desire to see Olga through other eyes than his [p. 193]. She bought him leather notebooks for his diaries and kept hers in children's exercise books. She put aside work on her own novel so that she could read Hegel and Heidegger and become an expert so that she could help Sartre with his theory. If she were interested in a person and there was even the slightest possibility that that person would not allow himself or herself to be drawn into Sartre's orbit and become a willing satellite, then de Beauvoir would not consider a separate friendship. Although she loved Nelson Algren, she gave him up because Sartre's life was more out of control than hers and it was clear that he needed her to manage it, to become his nurse. Not only did she take care of Sartre, his health, his women, his work, his meetings, she was expected also to take care of the "family" (Sartre's entourage), to organize their lives and to resolve all their difficulties. And . . . while doing all this, she wrote daily to Algren, telling him how wonderful he was. Even in the midst of writing *The Second Sex*, she put it aside to help Sartre work on the screenplay for *Dirty Hands*.

Then there was the issue of Sartre's women. By the time Simone de Beauvoir was 26, Sartre was hardly available to her sexually. He had started on a series of mistresses, a pattern which he would continue all his life. Not only did he insist that de Beauvoir accept this arrangement, but he would write her in graphic detail about all the physical and emotional elements of his affairs and would expect her approval and advice. He would also expect that she would include these mistresses in their circle of friends and "take care of them." If ever she were slow to give her approval or showed her jealousy, he became angry and critical. When he became tired of an affair, he used her as the "heavy" to break it up. In his later years, she routinely drove him from the home of one mistress to another's. Sartre had become like a Chinese landowner with his first, second, third, fourth mistresses, as he made his weekly rotations between Arlette and his other women.

In their political life, de Beauvoir again was not an equal but a handmaiden. Her biographer, Deidre Bair, states about her work with the RDE, the Ressemblement Démocratique Revolutionaire:

> However, the role she played and the way
> she was regarded in Sartre and Rouseel's
> party is typical of how she was treated
> by all of Sartre's political friends and
> allies. Everyone took it for granted
> that she had no convictions of her own
> and that all her positions she espoused
> were based on Sartre's. She could attend
> anything she wished, just so long as she
> was accompanying him or was sent by him.
> She was never invited independently to
> participate on any governing board or
> planning committee and, although she,
> sometimes, went alone to meetings Sartre
> could not attend, so she could report
> back to him, she was never considered his
> official representative, and was never
> really welcome without him. In political
> matters, she was truly La Grande
> Sartreuss, with no value or respect of
> her own.

The following is a comment from Italian scholar Anna Boschetti as she examines the roles of Sartre and de Beauvoir at *Les Temps Modernes* (the magazine he began):

> Simone de Beauvoir's trajectory is
> conditioned more than anyone else by her
> relationship to Sartre. It reflects the
> traditional sexist division of labor.
> Sartre develops existentialism,
> aesthetic, ethical and political

principles. His companion applies,
disseminates, clarifies, supports and
administers them.

Sartre rewarded this global devotion and sacrifice by, without de
Beauvoir's knowledge or agreement, deciding to adopt one of his last
mistresses, Arlette, as his daughter. In doing that, he left everything
he possessed to Arlette. De Beauvoir inherited nothing from Sartre. It
all belonged to Arlette. She had to beg Arlette to return the books that
had originally belonged to de Beauvoir's father, and she had to get
Arlette's permission to publish anything of Sartre's, including his
letters. In spite of this grand betrayal on Sartre's part, de Beauvoir
was so conditioned to disrespect, submission and abuse that she
agreed to be one of the sponsors of the adoption.

It is interesting that one becomes what one knows and what one
lives. When she began her relationship with Sylvie le Bon and
adopted her (yet another imitation of her mentor), this advocate of
women's equality, selfhood and independence encouraged Sylvie le
Bon to give up her career so that she would be free to travel with de
Beauvoir at a moment's notice, saying, "I have enough money for
both of us."

One of the men who knew her best, Nelson Algren, writes:

> The irony of *The Second Sex* is a purely
> literary irony. In reality, there was no
> irony. Second is where second belongs.
> It is still interesting to me how a woman
> may accept the secondary status of the
> second in a personal relationship and our
> personal relationship never got off that
> basis . . . I thought posterity ought to
> know that . . . she understood that in
> the relationship between a man and a
> woman, the man is the dominating factor
> specifically.

When de Beauvoir wrote an essay for *Flair*, espousing not a
master-slave relationship between the sexes but equality, Algren
asked her what all this "equality" bullshit was. She wrote to him, "No,

equality is only a myth. I only said you [men] were equal with me [women] to be polite. We'll achieve our field of equality this summer when we do the same thing at the same time."

So, sometimes, Simone de Beauvoir could utter the truth, could know and admit that she was not living an independent, authentic life and was not participating in "equal" relationships. "I can't speak of myself without speaking of him [Sartre]." When she spent weeks fussing over Nelson Algren, dropping all her New York friends and appointments, she knew she was acting "just like all the American women I had ridiculed for the way they catered to men's needs. The promises have all been kept. And yet, turning an incredulous gaze towards that young and credulous girl, I realize with stupor how much I was gypped." In *The Second Sex* de Beauvoir writes.

> Furthermore, like all the oppressed,
> woman deliberately dissembles her
> objective actuality; the slave, the
> servant, the indigent, all who depend
> upon the caprices of a master, have
> learned to turn toward him a changeless
> smile or an enigmatic impassivity; their
> real sentiments, their actual behavior
> are carefully hidden. [p 259]

About her affairs while she was supposed to be faithful to Sartre, de Beauvoir writes: "People expected me to be faithful so I pretended I was."

However, mainly and most of the time, de Beauvoir kept the myth alive through sheer stubbornness and determination to make the world accept her as the prototype of an individual, independent, self-actualized woman, to make the world accept her presentation of herself and Sartre as the successful couple with the idealized relationship. And the world—blind, gullible and easily seduced— accepted and perpetuated the non-truth, the myth, the lies, the fabrications.

Some "legends" have consciously and systematically set out to create a myth, knowing full well the dichotomy between what was truth and what needed to be perceived as truth. One such was President John F. Kennedy. As James N. Giglio tells us in his book

The Presidency of John Kennedy [University Press of Kansas], John F. Kennedy had a sickly childhood. He was born with an unstable back, contracted scarlet fever before his third birthday which weakened his overall condition. He suffered from asthma and from allergies and nearly died of diphtheria. By the time J.F.K. had reached twenty, he had colitis and a duodenal ulcer. By the time J.F.K. was pushed into politics by his father, it was known that he had Addison's disease and that he was in continual pain from a back injury. All that was kept in total secrecy. The pain became so acute at times that the President needed crutches to get around the White House. All his infirmities were most carefully concealed from public view. Concealed also were the times the pain became so excessive that he had to be lowered from planes in a wheelchair [p. 264].

To attempt to alleviate the suffering, President Kennedy received weekly injections of vaccine for his allergies. He was infected with corticosteroids for his Addison's disease and these exacerbated his growing intolerance of milk which aggravated a gastric disorder. He was also injected with amphetamines by Dr. Marc Jacobson-Dr. "Feel Good"—a man who in 1975 lost his medical license for more than thirty-five counts of unprofessional conduct. These amphetamine injections involved the possibility of addiction, hyperactivity, impaired judgment, increased irritability, hypertension and even psychosis.

All these facts were reiterated on a November 12, 1993 *20/20* program, where it was also exposed that thirty years after his death, all his medical records are not available, and where a tape was shown of his then White House physician, Janet Travell, assuring the American public that the President was in excellent health. The American public knew nothing about this. Very carefully, the President and his advisors conspired to present just the opposite image: a frontier image of touch football, fifty-mile hikes, golf, tennis, squash matches—a young man, virile and strong, in the prime of his life, striding coatless and hatless in 40° weather, conquering the universe. In truth, there was little capacity for strenuous physical activity, and what there was was severely limited—like having to learn to play golf with little involvement of back muscles and limited to nine holes. In truth, President Kennedy was in constant pain and needed to rely on a back brace, medications, massages, physical therapy just to get him through each day.

Another segment of the carefully created image was that of John F. Kennedy as a man of high intellect and considerable intellectual and creative capacity and accomplishment, a cultured and cultivated man, well-versed in the arts and nourished by them. His graduation thesis was published. His book about the PT-109 incident, *Profiles in Courage*, was awarded the Pulitzer Prize for biography. Articles with his byline appeared in *Look, American Heritage, Sports Illustrated.* Gala evenings in the White House included artists and performances by the most stellar names in music, drama, dance, opera. He was touted as an original thinker, a politician with strategies for America that were original and innovative and new.

In truth, President Kennedy was considered a mediocre and dilatory student. It is suspected that his thesis was published because Joe Kennedy asked *New York Times* journalist Arthur Krock to rewrite it and Henry Luce to compose a foreward and Krock's literary agent to secure a publisher. Again, Joe Kennedy pulled strings to get his son sea duty and to encourage the press to embellish Kennedy's activities at the destruction of PT-109 while ignoring the activities and contributions of others. It is suspected that he was instrumental in having an essay written about the incident and then ensuring mass distribution by using his influence to secure a *Reader's Digest* reprint. It is curious and interesting that there were no questions about the fact that the PT-109 incident was the only time a Japanese destroyer got so close to a PT boat. It is also suspected that *Profiles in Courage* was ghost-written. Certainly, it emerged that the research and draft had been done by several people: Ted Sorenson, Prof. Jules Davids of Georgetown University, etc. It also emerged that *Profiles in Courage* was not among the eight recommendations for the Pulitzer Prize in biography and, again, many believe that Joe Kennedy, through Arthur Krock, exerted an undue influence. The articles that appeared with his byline were all written by Ted Sorenson. And, despite his lavish White House galas for the arts, Kennedy knew little about painting, was bored by ballet and opera and was so engaged in his politics, his pain and his philandering that he had little time for a life of either the mind or the soul. His political ideas, rather than being original or innovative, evolved from President F.D. Roosevelt's Economic Bill of Rights address of January 11, 1944.

Yet one more touted image of the legend of Camelot was the notion of the perfect marriage, a marriage between two Hollywood-beautiful people, descended from high American, monied aristocracy, cultured, cultivated and special, with two adorable children, living a devoted and harmonious family life, with long idyllic family weekends featuring gleeful children and laughing parents. In reality, the President had numerous extramarital affairs which persisted throughout his presidency with anyone and everyone who either came to the White House when Jackie wasn't there or came to him through hotel secret passageways. In June, 1963 [p. 268], there were allegations that he had affairs with Suzy Chang and Marie Novotny, call girls from London and friends of Stephen Ward from the Profumo affair. Novotny shared a New York apartment with producer Harry Towers, a suspected Soviet agent who had fled the country in 1962. He was also reputed to have had affairs with East German model Ella Romasch, who provided favors to politicians and lobbyists, who had had an affair with a Soviet attaché and who was a suspected agent herself. He had affairs with Judy Campbell, who had had a liaison with the head of the Mob, Sam Giancana, Marilyn Monroe and with scores of others. The "blissfully" happy Mrs. Kennedy was often away from the White House for months at a time, traveling to Italy, India and Pakistan. She was unwilling to help her husband by assuming political obligations. She refused to meet with the Muscular Dystrophy Association, the American Red Cross, the Girl Scouts of America; she was very cool and uncommunicative with reporters and cancelled "political" engagements to go shopping and water skiing. It is rumored by those who knew her well that she was extremely insensitive to social issues, quarreled often and bitterly with the President, especially over her spending habits, and on numerous occasions contemplated divorce, only to be talked out of it by Joe Kennedy. The new Camelot, as the Camelot of old, was certainly disintegrating, if indeed it ever existed for even a moment in time.

But Kennedy, perhaps the most image-conscious president of this century, and his advisors knew what they had to do. He knew that image could conquer truth and personal style counter political ineptness. He took his two beautiful children, his glamorous wife, his own sex appeal and the informality of the rocking chair and photographed them and dispersed the images as often as possible. Like his father before him, he proceeded to "manage" the media. For television press conferences, Salinger prompted certain reporters to ask certain specific questions. During the Cuban crisis, Kennedy

117

asked the press to practice self-censorship. He proposed a media board to screen "dangerous" press stories. He asked the press to honor governmental reports not to print certain information. Arthur Sylvester argued that the news represented part of the "arsenal of weaponry" of the cold war, intimating that lying was acceptable in certain circumstances.

He was constantly scanning the newspapers for unfavorable comments and becoming enraged when he saw them. The President and his wife discontinued their weekly activities with Ben Bradlee and his wife for three months when there was a mildly critical observation about Kennedy and the press in *Look* magazine. In 1962, he cancelled twenty-two White House subscriptions to the Republican *New York Herald Tribune*.

At one point in time, J.F.K. agreed to meet with three leading journalists on national television to review the first half of his term. The media consented to first tape a long interview and then reduce it to an h our telecast. Kennedy deliberately gave the dullest answers to unfriendly questions, knowing that they would be dropped. George Herman called it a fascinating performance of skill.

It is ironic that legend rather than truth, myth rather than fact, continues into and beyond the Kennedy assassination. Could Lee Harvey Oswald along have killed the President? Could Jack Ruby alone have killed Oswald? J. Edgar Hoover pushed this theory through the F.B.I. The Warren Commission agreed. Yet the Commission used the F.B.I. and C.I.A. for investigation, agencies that had little interest in the truth. Some say that the F.B.I. needed to cover its tracks because it had failed to place Oswald on a security index, despite all they should have known about him. It is even possible that they employed him as an informant. He had connections with Cubans and organized crime. The C.I.A. had employed Mafia elements to assassinate Castro and they had to be concerned about embarrassing disclosures as relating to Cuban-connected conspiracy to kill Kennedy. It has been said by many who have studied the question that the Warren Commission overlooked leads, altered the testimony of witnesses, concealed information to make the reports conform to certain specifications. Testimony came from more than fifty witnesses who testified that they heard shots coming from the grassy-knoll area ahead of the motorcade. Seven reported smelling the odor of gunpowder in the same area. Because the President's body jerked backward and leftward, it suggests that he was also hit from right front. The Warren Commission neglected to explore the possibility of additional gunmen.

Numerous questions remain. Was Oswald a defector during his stay in the Soviet Union? To what extent was he tied to Mob chieftain Carlos Marcello? Was he pro- or anti-Castro? Was there someone who impersonated Oswald? Was he merely a patsy as he claimed to be before his death? Could he have successfully fired three shots in five to seven seconds? What were Jack Ruby's underworld connections from his Chicago days as Al Capone's runner? What about the more than a dozen witnesses who say that he and Oswald knew each other before the assassination? What about the evidence that Ruby was seen in various different places where Oswald was after the assassination, after he got a phone call from an underworld connection? Is the aftermath of the *image* of J.F.K.'s assassination as much a concoction of interested and desperate parties as were many aspects of the prince of Camelot and his reign?

We cast people in the images of gods. In doing that, we never know who they really are; we have no opportunity to collect all the information, know the truth and operate on the truth; we have no possibility of making a correct choice. We chose for the Presidency the image of Jack Kennedy, not the "real" Jack Kennedy. So we do ourselves a disservice by being active participants in the "emperor with no clothes" tale. Equally unproductive is that, in seeing others as gilded and unflawed, we see ourselves as lesser human beings and value less our own stature and our own worth.

Miriam Kove

MYTHS ABOUT DEATH

Is it not for us to confess that in our
civilized attitude towards death we are
once more living psychologically beyond
our means, and must reform and give truth
its due? Would it not be better to give
death the place in actuality and in our
thoughts which properly belongs to it,
and to yield a little more prominence to
the unconscious attitude towards death
which we have hitherto so carefully
suppressed? —S. Freud

In his Pulitzer Prize-winning book *The Denial of Death*, Ernest Becker contends that of all the things that move men, one of the principal ones is the terror of death. Animals, he says [p. 27], have no consciousness of death—a few minutes of fear, a few seconds of anguish and it is over. But man lives a whole lifetime with the idea that, at any given moment, his body may betray him, nature may betray him, circumstances may betray him, his fellow man may betray him (as I write, 23 cab drivers have been killed this year alone in New York City), and he will be extinguished from the face of the earth. Man lives a lifetime haunted by this grotesque fate and for many of us, our courage fails us and we attempt to drive ourselves into oblivion, into denial with social games, psychological tricks, personal preoccupations that are so removed from the reality of the situation that they are forms of madness.

For a person who works with children, it becomes eminently clear that all their symptoms are in some essential way connected to their fear of death. They feel themselves powerless in their ability to control the world, either in the global sense—psychiatrists reported an increase in anxiety neurosis in children as a result of the earth tremors in southern California [p. 23]—or in a finite personal sense—a child can't know what to do about a raging fever or a raging teacher. To deny this powerlessness, they attach themselves to a powerful heroic figure (usually the parent) to whom they ascribe omnipotent magical powers over all things, and who, for a price, will protect them from and control for them all the terrifying possibilities and vicissitudes of a dreaded and demonic world. Most of us never outgrow this situation. Repressing our annihilation dread and our sense of hopelessness, we have an inner urge to merge ourselves with power figures who will protect us against the callous unconcerns of nature. We become dependent children blindly following the voice of the powerful parent, hoping to get back to the magical protection, the participation in omnipotence, the "oceanic" feelings which we once enjoyed. We ascribe to those power figures godlike capacities, grant them total devotion (masochistic submission) and, as their followers, participate in their godlike powers. Already we are living in a delusion, for though adults (hopefully) have some measure of competence and ability to function, they are, of course, not omnipotent, and when it emerges that they can't protect us from whopping cough or from accidents or from neighborhood bullies or dysfunctional school personnel or from the baser aspects of their own nature, we, the children, are left at a loss. How do we explain this state of affairs and the relentless terror and helplessness that it engenders? We blame ourselves. Certainly, they are the gods we know them to be and can manage all the magical, fantastical tasks of control, but we have been "bad" and because of our "badness," we have caused these deities to punish us or not to interfere with man and nature on our behalf. It is thus that we develop self-blame, self-hatred and that low sense of self-esteem that is the core and center of many of our life difficulties.

Recently, I had occasion to call one of my child patients to cancel a session because I had sprained my back. He listened very carefully to my explanation and then said, "Are you my friend?" The message behind the words was: "Please tell me that I'm OK, that I didn't cause the misfortune and that you're not angry with me." When I repeated these feelings back to him and reassured him that this situation was definitely not caused by him, there was a large sigh and a jubilant "OK." This boy had worked very hard in three years of treatment to be able to know and acknowledge these feelings and ideas. What of the others?

When we become adults and it becomes evident, at least to our conscious selves, that our parents are simply human, how then do we handle the conscious or unconscious terror of death? We are now, at least on some level, aware that our kin are not omnipotent, but the dread of death continues to exist and so does the inner urge to merge ourselves with power figures who will protect us against the callous unconcern of nature and who will assimilate our need to merge and lose ourselves in something larger.

One solution for many people is religion. Certainly God, Jesus Christ is conceived as omnipotent and omniscient, able to love us, protect us, feed us (Jesus and the fishes), limit us (witness all the rules and regulations as to how we are to conduct ourselves in life) and abandon and destroy us (Job) or raise us to heights of impossible and unforeseen victory (David, the Maccabees, the spread of Christianity). In God, we have found the all-powerful Other, more powerful than our parents, since he is alien and not even of our species, who can not only shine munificence to us on earth and protect us from earthly death until we are very old, but who can protect us from death at all by the idea of an afterlife, an idea that we never truly die but simply change form as we proceed to another chapter of life. What better way of keeping the terror of death at bay than by denying its ultimate existence in the theory of immortality. I am not here trying to suggest that there is no afterlife. Perhaps there is. As a human being, I am finite. My knowledge is finite and there are many aspects of the universe which I know not of, many unknowables which may someday be knowable. I am suggesting that in the many strands that weave together to account for human actions, one of these, at least, is the search for the ultimate omnipotent parent. It is not a coincidence that God and Jesus Christ and Allah are often referred to as Father, that the Pope is addressed as Our Holy Father and that priests also are given that appellation.

It was very much my experience when I worked as a clinician and intake director at the Institutes of Religion and Health that people who came for therapy there were seeking an intervention for themselves, an apostle of Norman Vincent Peale, who would intercede for them with God and thus have their miseries cease and their prayers answered. Like children, they waited for the Other to love them, protect them and give them what they needed. Initially, it was amazing to me how little concept there was of self-responsibility, how little belief there was in creating and sustaining one's own life, how little credence was given to one's own will. These people felt helpless and powerless in themselves, terrified in their essence, and their only hope was the intercession and benevolence of God. When that did not come, like children they took the blame unto themselves and hated themselves for the "sins" they had committed in thought or deed that kept them from God's love and bounty. They often spoke of preachers and evangelists and radio personalities who exhorted them to put their life into God's hands and all would be well. These are dynamics that I have come to know well among religious populations, whether they be orthodox Jews or devout Mohammedans—a delivering oneself into the hands of the powerful Other as a means of escaping not only one's own sense of perplexity, helplessness and incompetence in the face of life but especially the haunting of the days and nights of that life by the fate of death. Together with this deliverance into the hands of the Other goes a striving for "goodness," behavior conforming to the rules made by the representatives of natural power as a way of winning their approval.

It goes without saying that the price we pay for this denial of death is our not allowing ourselves to grow up, to be the masters of our fate, to develop authentic lives forged out of considered aims and morals and values, lives uniquely our own which we shape and live wholeheartedly and for which we take responsibility, but we remain children, helpless and powerless, dependent on the bounty and abuse, on the whim of the other or Other. A client of mine who had systematically been sexually abused since the age of ten was convinced consciously that her present misery and depression were directly related to and punishment for those "sins" that she had committed. She unconsciously pursued men and situations that would hurt her and defeat her, both as repetitions of her early experiences and as "atonement" of her sins. Another was shamed and humiliated by every "bad" thought he had—not even "bad" thoughts were allowed in his strict Roman Catholic home. A third very intelligent and talented woman totally ignored her own life while ministering to two severely ill relatives on separate coasts because that was what God would want her to do.

For the non-religious among us, the denial of death often takes the form that Ernest Becker describes as the Romantic solution. Our parents have become humanly flawed, God is thought of as impossible, inaccessible, unknowable, too unpredictable, and so the love partner becomes the divine ideal within which to fulfill one's life. All one's security, spiritual and moral needs become fixed in one individual.

Just yesterday, I listened to a very expressive young woman with pleading eyes and multiple hand gestures describe that at 30, she knew that she didn't feel passionate about her boyfriend but that she married him because she knew that he was responsible and stable and that he would "take care of" her. Another young woman, long married, miserable in her marriage, unable to leave it because of her fear that she was unable to cope alone, started an affair and after the third date reported with a sigh of great relief and satisfaction that she thought that this man was "serious" about her, that he was willing to become the new head of the household and "look after" her and her children. A very intelligent and sophisticated man, a high-priced executive, reported feeling, during a halftime period in a football game when the cheerleaders appeared, suddenly bereft, empty, totally depressed, wishing he had a gun so that he could "shoot [his] brains out." He very correctly traced this sudden depression to underlying annihilation dread that was constant and pervasive whenever he realized that he didn't have a special woman in his life. Yet another young woman gave a business and herself into the hands of a married man because he had promised he would "rescue" her. All her life she had felt "adrift," alone, unable (gifts and reality to the contrary) to believe that she could create and sustain her own life in this world, and now she had finally found the "Divine Other" who could wipe away her existential fears and in whom she could lose herself in her total financial and emotional yielding. She left treatment so she would not have to "see" the impossibility of her position. Again and again, in our society and in our lives, we experience people running headlong into the Romantic solution.

In *Pretty Woman*, a prostitute, having nothing and going nowhere in her life, was rescued by Richard Gere, who represented the rich and powerful other, eminently able to negotiate the practical world, who would presumably negotiate it for her. She, being labile and expressive and childish, would rescue him from the Yuppie straightjacket. Each would become the romantic solution of the other, and neither needed to be responsible for the creation of a more human and autonomous self. *White Palace*, where a repressed, confused Yuppie and a lovely, angry child-woman "save" each other, is a different version of a similar theme.

The lover becomes deified, becomes "the springtime," "the "angel glow," "the sun in the morning and the moon at night," the "lucky star," "my everything." The love object is the divine perfection and one's own self is elevated by joining one's own destiny to it.

From Shakespeare's *Sonnets*:

> But thy eternal summer shall not fade
> Nor lose possession of that fair thou ow'st,
> Nor shall Death brag thou wand'rest in his shade
> When in eternal lines to time thou grow'st.
> So long as men can breathe or eyes can see,
> So long lives this, and this gives life to thee.
>
> But if the while I think on thee, dear friend,
> All losses are restored and sorrows end.
>
> His beauty shall in these black lines be seen,
> And they shall live and he in them still green.
>
> Nor Mars his sword nor war's quick fire shall burn
> The living record of your memory.
> 'Gainst death and all oblivious enmity
> Shall you pace forth; your praise shall still find
> room
> Even in the eyes of all posterity
> That wear the world out to the ending doom.
> So, till the judgment that yourself arise,
> You live in this, and dwell in lovers' eyes.

Many of us have had the experience either of meeting many people who have no friends, only social acquaintances, and often no concept of friendship. If we have an opportunity to explore this phenomenon, we hear numerous explanations—the person is too shy to make friends; has no time to make friends; can't find people who have his interests or his philosophy in life; doesn't feel that others know how to be friends; feels that others are interested only in their own well-being and will eventually abandon and betray you . . . While there is a kind of validity in all these rationalization, the fundamental truth generally emerges to be that these people have no friends because they *need* no friends because, in their organization or experience, their salvation lies not possibly in anyone else but only in the Romantic Solution. Only the Prince can rescue you on a white horse and transport you from the wicked stepmother. Only he can give you the beautiful palace with the attendant perfect life, so why concern yourself with the other peasants in the feudal village? In the opposite gender rescue myth, only the substitute mommy can make you feel loved and admired and worthwhile and sexually potent and satisfied while feeding, protecting and comforting you at the same time, so why bother with the other boys and girls at the church social or around the water cooler?

Many of us have had the experience of being suddenly and unceremoniously abandoned by a friend the moment a husband, wife or significant other has entered that friend's life. It's not that we've suddenly become ugly, stupid, boring, worthless. It's that we're simply wiped out when the longed-for solution arrives, the Romantic Solution.

The Romantic Solution embodies within it very serious difficulties. It cannot hold. However we might idealize and idolize our human partner, he inevitably must reflect earthly decay and imperfection. The Omnipotent Other is constantly evidencing, through sickness, failure, absence, that he or she is not in total control and that we are thus not totally safe and protected. Since, unconsciously, we can't hear that because it raises specters of our own annihilation, either we are faced with expending great psychic energy in denial, in lying to ourselves and maintaining our myth, or we feel great waves of rage and hopelessness, self-blame, abandonment, depression and suicidal thoughts. If we opt for the former, we put ourselves in the dependent, masochistic position of fawning and twisting to please and pleasure the love object and gain his or her approval. Thus, we have to deflate ourselves to keep the relationship, even if we glimpse the impossibility of it and the slavishness to which it reduces us. Often the "god" partner cannot stand it. He cannot stand the burden of "godhood" and so he must resent the slave. Then—how can he be a genuine god if the slave is so miserable and unworthy?

If a person is anointed a God, he or she can move easily towards becoming the Devil. An abused, beaten, victimized woman "cannot" leave her husband because, though he has become the devil, the power of her "living" still resides in him. A sexually abused child, though able in reality to "tell" others and get real help, feels that he or she can't because no one else has the total power of the omnipotent devil. Thus, we suffer the mutilation of our bodies and the skewing of our lives for the promise of "survival."

Most precisely, it takes away from us *responsibility for our own life*. This feels comfortable. Is our life difficult and painful? We can lay it at our partner's feet. Is the sense of being a separate individual trying to make some sense of life, of who one is, too confusing and frustrating? One can wipe it away in an emotional yielding to the partner. However, the partner really represents the negation of one's own distinctive personality, the negation of the courage to muddle and stumble and search for a unique self to stand alone in freedom.

An alternate solution to the problem of annihilation anxiety is to throw oneself under the hypnotic spell of a "leader." We put our judgment and common sense aside and once more become dependent children blindly following the voice of the parents, transferred now, not onto God or onto the romantic ideal but onto some "heroic" figure. We abandon our egos to his, identify with his power, and try to function with him as an ideal. The members of a group surrounding a "heroic" leader or chief do not feel that they are alone with their own smallness and helplessness as they share in the powers of the hero leader with whom they identify. The realities of the world—that man is a small trembling animal who will die, that the economic realities foster hunger and deprivation, that one country cannot fight many— are put aside and the illusion taken on that the leader is omnipotent and can assure victory over impossible odds, and that by participating in his powers, they can become heros, vital to the universe, immortal in some way. Thus the Germans believed that Hitler could lead them to world victory and economic greatness; the Iranians believed that the Ayatollah could make the world Muslim; Husssein's followers, on the eve of desecration, are not yet convinced that they have lost; Jim Jones' followers traveled into unknown destinations to set up an impossible community. We "suspend our disbelief" for the reward of participating in the glorious, immortal powers of the chief.

To me, the cults are a perfect example of this transference to a leader. Often adolescents, or emotional adolescents, needing to separate themselves from the parents because of age-appropriate urges or rage or disillusionment and yet unable to face the task of taking responsibility for their own life, find a leader to follow who, for them, will embody the idealized parent, so different from the human parent they've rejected, and will, thus, allay their unconscious terror of individuation and death. At the same time, because they rationalize this as an adult choice, it allows them to feel grown up and deny the dependent, infantile underpinnings for their choice. I recently saw a perfect and eccentric example of this dynamic. A young man, directly pursuant to the death of his father, left his job and his wife and joined the Moonies.

Besides providing a magical merger, a leader also provides for the members of the group the possibility of forbidden impulses, secret wishes and fantasies. In group behavior, anything is OK because the leader approves it. Thus, murder can be justified, as can incestuous or promiscuous sex, either because the leader has transformed it and made it "holy" as in a holy way or because it is the leader who is seen as taking responsibility for the act and not the individual members of the group. How many Germans "explained" their grotesque acts as "simply obeying" their leader? And how many; of Hussein's soldiers are on public TV exonerating their acts because they were "forced" to them by their chief? Manson's family explained their butchery and sexual practices by saying that they knew that he was God and that only by following through his plans could they be saved. Their leader was a holy hero and those who destroy on his command are no longer murderers but holy heroes. Thus, in the psychology of the group cult, the individual participants are provided not only with a depository of their omnipotent wish for immortality but with acting—out of their infantile sexual and aggressive fantasies. Participation in the group allows for the denial of everyday reality and its replacement with an aura of the sacred . . . and the false.

The groups use the leader with regard to fulfilling their infantile needs and urges. What they give up in this pursuit is their freedom to individual thought, conscience, choice, experience. The leader is as much a creature of the group as they of him [Becker, p. 136], and thus he loses his individual distinctiveness by being a leader, as they do by being his followers. No one has the freedom to be himself. Because the group and the leader share a common delusion, they are doomed to destruction because reality inevitably steps in and has its own way. Thus, pragmatically, the plans of these groups not only do not bear fruition in everyday life, but the members are doomed to disillusionment in the leader's persona itself, either in the imperfections that invariably surface or in his death and lack of immortality. Nasser, Lenin . . .

A yet third "solution" to the problem of fear of death is the artist's use of his art as a road to personal immortality, his own "beyond." Yes, he as a living creature, a "natural" creature, may have to submit to extinction, but his work will endure and he will endure in his art.

> . . . The living record of your memory.
> 'Gainst death and all oblivious enmity
> Shall you pace forth; your praise shall still find room
> Even in the eyes of all posterity
> That wear the world out to the ending doom.
> So, till the judgment that yourself arise,
> You live in this, and dwell in lovers' eyes.

Shakespeare is, in this sonnet, assuring his love that he/she will never die because he/she has been immortalized by the endurance of the work of art. Implicit in this statement is the endurance of the artist himself/herself. His—the artists'—creative work is a result of his own unique gifts, his own personal immortality and "private religion" [Becker, p. 172].

However, this solution, like the others, presents problems. First, he is still a creature and even if the work survives, he will not. He will not escape the actual fate of all mortal men. He has the same fears and anxieties about his actual life ending as do all mortal men. Second, how does he know that his art is good, that it will endure? Perhaps it is really bad, meaningless, incomprehensible. Perhaps it is "good" but the outside world will not recognize its "goodness." Perhaps the world will not recognize the new meanings the artist is introducing into the world. And what of the work of art itself? It is material. It is visible. It can spoil, tarnish, disintegrate, get lost, go out of fashion. And—no matter how splendid it is, it "still pales next to the transcending majesty of nature; and so it is ambiguous, hardly a solid immortality symbol. In his greatest genius man is still mocked" [Becker, p. 172]. So in achieving his specialness in creation, the artist must ultimately admit his own "creatureliness."

For those of us who are not artists, not religious, not romantic, we unconsciously attempt to find solutions in neurosis. If we carefully examine the nature and motive of neurotic symptoms, it soon becomes evident that very often the symptom is evidence and defense of that we are in terror of and that the specific fear is merely an offshoot of the more general fear of death. For example, a patient comes in and relates that she has met a very attractive man on her job, that he has asked her out and that she has refused. What emerges in the session is that she has been so abused by her former husband and her father that she cannot yet again put herself in a "vulnerable" position with men. Probing further, great sadness surfaces, and then anger, and then a feeling of being "lost" and "empty," all related to her father's abandonment when she was three—and finally, she is in touch with the terror of feeling left and knowing that she didn't know what to do or how to do it or how to exist alone in this world. Another patient is five and afraid to go to school. Her father has died and her fear of school is related not to anything horrible happening in the school but to her need to stay home and watch her mother constantly to ascertain that her mother is alive. Without mother, she is dead and that is not to be borne. Yet another person I see is hypochondriacal. Every physical symptom is experienced as a horrendous trauma and is immediately brought to one or more doctors. A mother who became terrified and hysterical at every childhood illness precipitated a grown-up equally terrified of every physical symptom and the possibility of death. Some people don't fly and some people avoid elevators. Some people wash their hands fourteen times per hour. Some men "flash"; some people so repress their feelings that they march around like automatons. Mainly the repressed feelings have to do with a deeply held sense of danger of dying, or drowning, of being cast adrift to perish. They may be overlaid by rage or sadness or confusion or frustration, but the most toxic, denied feelings are those connected with dread of annihilation. Every symptom is specific and unique to the individual, his experiences and the fashion in which he has organized these experiences. Yet every symptom is an attempt to defend against anxiety, to bind the anxiety, the whole blood of terror of dying. What depression, addiction, sado-masochism, perversions . . . and their unique symptoms have in common is an underlying sense of helplessness and hopelessness, an inability to perform adequately enough in the world to be safe and a desperate attempt to keep this knowledge at bay.

Freud outlined a hierarchy of children's terrors: (1) fear of annihilation, (2) fear of loss of the object, (3) fear of loss of the love of the object . . . As becomes immediately evident, they are all phases of the dread of death, phases that persist in us long after we chronologically outlive our childhood.

The ironic truth about neurosis is that as the person seeks to avoid death, he does so by killing off so much of himself, skewing so much of himself and so large a piece of his action-world, that he is isolating himself, diminishing himself and becoming as though dead. How many of us have met people who "function" but who have no real access to who they are, what they want, what they feel? How many of us have met people who know who they are and what they want and what they feel but who hide and isolate themselves from others because of fear of deadly repercussions in exposure? How many of us are so terrified to be proven wrong and incompetent that we risk nothing, venture nothing and achieve very little? How many of us hate others because we really hate ourselves?

Neurosis is a series of lies we tell ourselves about the world. The first lie is to so skew our behavior and our reality that we can feel safe in the world. That is a large piece of man's real madness that he attempts to deny his true condition. This is not a safe world and we are not safe in it. Second, we lie to ourselves when we envision ourselves as powerless and hopeless in the existential disaster. We are not. We are intelligent beings with competence and some control in managing the world. We need not organize ourselves as passive objects, a plaything of the world, but as active centers within ourselves—creators and sustainers of our own lives.

Most of us can't manage that. We are terrified and we need desperately to defend against the "human perplexity and helplessness in the face of nature's dreadful faces," "the painful riddle of death" [Freud]. We do that in the personal ways already explored and other means that become institutionalized—societal neurosis or institutionalized pathology, methods and means that become a national way of life and a national means of coping with fear of death.

The men of the Chagga tribe wear an anal plug all their lives [Becker, p. 32]. This is a pretense to have sealed up the anus and not to need to defecate. This is their attempt to triumph over the physical, over their realization that they are of nature and that, as for everything in nature, death awaits. For centuries, women have undergone numerous restrictions and taboos because, due to their menstrual cycle and their birthing abilities, they are perceived as reminders of man's "naturalness." Thus, in certain tribes, women are secreted in huts during menstruation. In the Jewish religion, they are removed from men to their own sequestered part of the synagogue, and as Marilyn French says in her book, *Division of Experience*, "eventually the hard circumstances of human life led to a valuing of control over and separation from nature as an absolute good and a defining human characteristic. As this sense of things developed, women's supposed closeness to nature became a stigma rather than a miracle, and woman began to be seen as lower than man; being part of nature in the way that men were not, they were also part of what must be controlled." Women in the synagogue were sequestered to their own part so they might not tempt men or contaminate them with their uncleanness.

In our own society we do many things as a group to allay our terror. We tranquilize ourselves with the trivial. Modern man is drinking, eating, drugging and shopping himself out of awareness. By keeping constantly busy, moving and acquiring, we can keep our terror at bay because we give ourselves no moment to consider. We lift our faces, color our hair, staple our stomachs, exercise ourselves without mercy, all in the hope that if we continue to look young, then we will be young and death will not find us out. If looking young is not enough, we attach ourselves to someone who is young. Every year, thousands of men throw away their middle-aged wives and turn them in for a new model, a twenty-five year old, a twenty-two year old. Being with youth is their magic talisman against creeping age, decay and death. Rank tells us that the death fear of the ego is loosened by the killing, the sacrifice of the other. One buys oneself off from the penalty of dying or being killed. Perhaps that is why so many middle-aged men not only abandon their wives but try to kill them off emotionally and financially. Our obsession with health foods and macrobiotic diets and nutritionists, etc. is a continuous search for the prevention of death, for discovery of the fountain of youth, timelessness and agelessness.

On Broadway at the moment of this writing, we find *The Secret Garden, City of Angels, Carousel*. The movie marquees herald *Home Alone, Sleeping with the Enemy, The Object of Beauty, Four Weddings and a Funeral, Reality Bites, Bad Girls*. All these depict and concern young people, falling in love, falling out of love, killing one another, betraying one another. Our over-fifty actors and actresses have disappeared. There is no place for them to go, no place for them to work. No one seems to acknowledge that older people have lives of interest, of merit, of struggle, of success and blooming and surprise and development and sickness and loss. No one wants to acknowledge that older people live, that they contribute, that they have news to bring to us, things to share with us and educate us about. No one wants to acknowledge them, period. We don't want to talk about aging, loss, illness, dying. We don't want to know. If the mirror we hold up to nature reflects the young and the beautiful, then we can mesmerize ourselves into believing that we can stay young and beautiful. I recently saw *Hamlet* and was enormously perturbed by the juxtaposition of appearance between Hamlet and Gertrude. Hamlet, played by Mel Gibson, in closeup had very visible lines and wrinkles in his face, on his forehead, around his eyes, his mouth. Yet Glenn Close, as his mother, had not one single line or wrinkle on the snow white perfection of her visage. Was she perhaps too young to play Hamlet's mother? Surely, an older actress would have been more appropriate, less obviously ludicrous, but clearly the director, a man probably in his 60s, wanted youth and beauty, even at the cost of ludicrousness in appropriateness.

It has always seemed whimsical and sad to me to read the personal ads and to see that women are thrown away at 45. Before 45, a woman might still be considered viable and vibrant—a possibility. At the magical age of 46, she becomes a relic, an impossibility as a candidate for love, sex, romance, marriage. It would be interesting to do a study of personal ads to see what percentage solicit women over 45. Probably 1%. Perhaps the man is 49 or 59 or 69, but a 46 year old woman is too close to death for him, too much a statement of reality. Oh, he can admire and even lust after Joan Collins or Linda Evans or Jane Fonda or Michele Lee or Donna Mills, all of whom are more than fifty. But they have all had face lifts and stomach tucks and . . . so that we can pretend that they're young and we can all live happily ever after in the myth.

And what about our superheroes—Batman, Superman, Flash Gordon, Rambo, The Terminator? They meet all, they conquer all. No matter how difficult the environment, how evil the genius, how numerous the enemy, they conquer. Is this not the popular illusion that we can conquer all and, by association, death itself as well?

I believe that it is real madness to deny our true condition. We come from dust and we return to dust. We all, no matter how beautiful, gifted, moneyed, esteemed, artistic, *must*, sooner or later, die. Perhaps we go to heaven, to a place of wonder and unspeakable bliss, of light and profound beauty; perhaps we return to earth in some different form and live again. Perhaps there is only cessation of sensation and nothingness. To erect structures based on fantasies and wishes and fears is understandable but unknowable and unproductive. What we do know is that we die, that most of us don't want to die and that most of us are afraid to die.

Once we can acknowledge our fear of death, we no longer need to suppress it. We embrace it, we accept it and we live with it as we pursue with energy and vitality our present existence. One of the wisdoms is to acknowledge that there are areas of life we can control, others we control not at all and still others over which we have only some control. As the adage remind us, it's important to know the difference, to place your energies on that where control is possible and to accept with grace and resignation that which you can't control—or with anger; as Dylan Thomas says, "Do not go gentle into the good night . . . Rage, rage against the dying of the light." Rage if you must, but know that the "dying of the light" comes to all of us and we can't wish it away with obsessional delusions. Let us stop lying to ourselves and admit our mortality.

Once we have done that, we need to have the courage to stand alone in freedom, to know that each one of us is a painfully separate person with only ourself to lean on. It is we who are responsible for and need to take charge of our own lives and do the best we can with them. It is not God or a parent or a lover or a boss or a priest or a guru or a President. Living with the possibility of aging, falling ill, being injured, being crushed, being annihilated, we must consent every day to give ourselves up to the risks and dangers of the world, allow ourselves to be engulfed and used up as we strive to understand who we authentically are, what we really want out of this life, by what principles we conduct ourselves in this world, and then proceed with what courage we can muster to act, to build a life on the foundations of that knowledge. Mental illness is people who have lost the courage to separate, to grow up, to accept the burden and responsibility for their own life. Does that mean that we are alone? On some level, we are. The hard choices, the hard work of our life is ours. Whose life is it, anyway? Your own. On some level, we are not alone. There are relatives and friends and lovers and husbands and children and benevolent strangers, and we can offer each other love and support and empathy and physical help, and we must strive to be at ease not only with being able to be separate but also with being able to unite. It takes courage also to be dependent and to be dependent sometimes is very healthy. Life is a ballet in which we wander alone through a beautiful, mysterious forest, stopping to breathe the air, to think our thoughts, to identify the foliage, to interact with the prince, the wood nymphs, the villagers, the wicked fairy. It is not a story told by an idiot signifying nothing, but a feast for the soul and the senses. We need to hear the music, to feel the breeze, to delight in the beauty, to savor the love, to struggle with the fairy, to absorb it all and explore it and ponder it and savor it and bow gracefully at the final curtain and retire to know that we've had our moment in the spotlight and it did not find us wanting and that that moment may be the sum of our allotment.

Why am I making so much of these myths, and so very many others, that we learn at our parents' knee, these lies that are woven into the fabric of our society and into the skein of our consciousness? Because they affect adversely every aspect of our lives, every one of our efforts to deal with the present and our capacity to deal with the future.

Practically, if one doesn't have the realistic facts about a problem, the precise and adequate data of information regarding an issue, when one attempts to handle the problem and find a working solution, one will fail. For example, consider former Mayor Koch's plan to address the homeless situation in New York City. At conservative count, there were approximately hundreds of thousands of homeless in New York. For all of these, the mayor had 4 units that combed the city and attempted to observe the homeless, to evaluate their propensity to harm themselves or others and to hospitalize those who showed these tendencies. How many myths was the mayor creating? First, there is the myth that 4 units of 4 people can oversee hundreds of thousands of people. Beginning with this lie, we are already doomed to failure. However, other breaks with reality follow fast on this one. Are the civil liberties of this population being violated, and if they are, will we not have many Billie Boggs cases, and should we not first, then, try to establish some new laws that address these issues? Second, by saying that we have to evaluate these people to understand whether they are capable of harming themselves, are we then not perpetuating a second myth? Perhaps these people are not, in the main, overtly suicidal, but is not the fact that they are living on the streets, often in freezing temperatures, in cardboard boxes, not sufficient testament to the fact that they are not adequately well-functioning to maintain themselves in any productive and healthy way and that they need long-term treatment and many auxiliary services if they are to be able to lead decent lives? As a clinician, I was quite frankly infuriated with the lawyers of the ACLU and the media for disseminating the idea that Ms. Boggs was "healthy." Every intelligent person who is rational and objective and not prejudiced and self-serving would have to recognize that a human being who is lying on street corners is not emotionally healthy. I was not at all surprised to hear later evidence of Ms. Boggs' psychotic behavior. Yet, here we were pretending on a global scale, and nary a comment from the American Psychological Association or the American Medical Association, etc. After "picking up" people in this inadequate fashion, based on lie and deception, they are then confined to a special patient unit where they are treated for forty-eight days and then discharged. The myth would be that they have then been rehabilitated to society. What utter deception. Again, every decent clinician will know that it is impossible to rehabilitate people with such excessive damage in forty-eight days. They would need follow-up pharmacological and therapeutic treatment of long duration, careful case management, one-on-one supervision, placement in special homes or halfway houses. Instead, they are released. Many of them, of course, return to the street corners, to Central Park, to vagrancy and despair. A worker in charge of these hospital placements was not embarrassed on a TV program to say that some of these homeless people are discharged into SROs, when we know that SROs are the pits of purgatory. Thus, we had a mayor who was myth-making about our homeless population and, in so doing, was relegating all of us to a dismal present and a terrifying future.

How are we myth-making about our drug problem? Are we discussing and exploring and understanding the etiology of drug abuse-the various strands that lead people to drug use such as feelings of emptiness, inadequacy, deadness, terror of being abandoned and dying, a need for drugs to soothe and comfort oneself? Are we treating our children and our adults so that we can diagnose them early and treat them adequately? Are we setting up good schools and caretaking facilities where our kids will learn self-respect and self-regulation? Are we organizing drug treatment clinics in every community so that help is available and affordable? Is our law enforcement really vigorously pursuing large drug dealers and small drug dealers and every drug dealer? Is our country putting every possible punitive pressure on countries that are exporting drugs? Are the big business corporations divesting themselves of interests from people and companies and countries associated with drug trafficking? Is there a well-endowed, carefully appointed task force to consider and investigate this vital issue in all its complexities, including the possibility of legalizing drugs? No. What we have, amid rumors of the government of our own country being involved in Iranian drug operations, is our former First Lady appearing on television and asking our children to "say no to drugs." The myth the government is creating—the lie they are propagating—is that one lady—who means nothing to many of us, who is negatively perceived by others of us—can in a sixty-second commercial make any difference in so complex and widespread and disastrous a problem. Thus, we are spending and wasting money and our time as we watch the problem of drug abuse escalating, as we see hundreds and thousands of people shattered and destroyed by the impact. The problem worsens as we teach our citizens how to be self-serving, image-making and totally ineffective while paying no attention to the truth that would set us free, addressing the reality of the problem and diving into the think tank for the productive solutions that would make a difference.

Several weeks ago, a new patient of mine brought me in a book to read about couples. She was in the midst of a recent separation, desperately wanting to get back with a husband who did not want to get back with her; searching for every possible ray of hope, she had found this book. I took it home to read and was astounded. This book was written by a couple who not only themselves had written several previous books but were also running groups all over the country, counseling couples in attaining better relationships. The book was crazy-making. It perpetuated a series of myths which was absolutely contrary to the reality of how people function, how they relate and what is productive for them. The myths ran the spectrum from advocating, totally, in oneself, the negation of negative feelings to claiming that one person alone could make and control a relationship, to advocating no acknowledgement of the other's differences but pretending that the two partners were as one. I saw at once that this book was based on the authors' serious emotional problems, a fantasy of symbiotic harmony, a fantasy of omnipotent control, a fantasy of twinship, etc. The authors were using their own neurosis to create a myth of relationship and disseminating this myth into the unsuspecting community. The people who read the book and tried the system, the people who attended the workshops, were (1) wasting their money; (2) wasting their time and energy; (3) bound to fail, since all the underpinnings of this system were wrong and with a very faulty foundation, the building cannot hold. Allegorically, the authors were advocating that people construct a two-story structure on a firm foundation of marshmallows. (4) The people who were well-meaning but ignorant and looking for expert help would come away not only with failure but also with shame and guilt and feelings of hopelessness and inadequacy since obviously they had failed in a task where they were told it was totally within their own power to succeed.

This total skewing of reality leading to failure in productive living as well as self-blame and shame and confusion and frustration is typical of the residue of the dissemination and perpetuation of myth. In their total discounting of the tenets of reality, of what is real and what is not in terms of how people function in themselves and with others, these authors were not only exhibiting their own madness but perpetuating it outwards into the community.

Several days ago, I saw an eighteen year old boy for a consultation. He had returned home after two months of his first year of college. While there, he had been severely depressed, unable to function and do the required work. Hysterical and hopeless, he had returned home. What emerged in the consultation was that he considered himself as a failure now and knew that he would forever be a failure due to his inability to handle the college situation. Somewhere, somehow, he had integrated the myth that he must immediately do well at anything he attempted or he was a failure and lost. No other alternatives were possible in his vocabulary of the world. For two hours, he sobbed in self-abuse and self-flagellation for the scum that he was. It took many hours of treatment for him to be able to see that "failure" is a "normal" aspect of living, that a problem has solutions, that he wasn't "bad" for being human instead of a perfectly succeeding automaton and that there were many wonderful options and possibilities in his future life.

A six year old came into the playroom and squealed with joy at the fingerpaints. She just knew they would be there today. How did she know that, since there had been no fingerpaints in the playroom since we had started to work and she had never mentioned the idea to me? She had wished and wished for them, and her mom had told her that when she wanted something badly she should wish for it and it would come true. Certainly this mother loved her child. Certainly she did not want to skew her development and her sense of reality testing. But she did. In teaching her child this myth—this lie—that most probably was taught to her, she had opened up her child's life to endless disappointment when wishes did not come true, a sense of failure since she, the child, must obviously be doing something wrong if she was not getting results from something her mother assured her would bring results, and a potential sense of great guilt when she wished for negative occurrence such as harm to a playmate, punishment to parents, etc.

Last night in a conversation with my daughter, she related an incident of meeting a new school counselor and how "nice" he was. When I asked her how she knew that he was "nice," she thought carefully for a few moments and then said that he complimented her on her appearance, smiled a lot and seemed very warm. We then proceeded to have a fairly lengthy discussion about the difference between "charm" and "niceness"—which basically is decent, concerned, warm, ethical behavior. I had come across this counselor many times as a professional colleague and knew him to be, unfortunately, a manipulative, self-centered, unethical, power-hungry man who, like so many psychopaths, had an extremely charming, seductive surface. Somehow, my daughter had learned a societal myth: that an ingratiating surface indicated a decent human being.

These myths—whether personal, familiar, societal or global—are all basically lies, lies that we have been taught to regard as truths. They skew our reality testing, make it impossible to understand what is really present, what is really happening, thus making it impossible for us to deal with a situation, solve a problem, small or large, because we don't have the correct data, the proper pieces, the right instruments to put the puzzle together and solve it.

To be grossly allegorical, let us assume that you wore a special pair of glasses that made every table appear to be an automobile. You would bring your dining room table out into your driveway and you would attempt to drive it. No matter how hard you tried, how good a driver you were or how much first-rate gasoline you put into the table, it would not move down the highway. You would be doomed to frustration, confusion, failure and hopelessness despite your considerable intelligence and your best efforts. Of course, if you alone had that special pair of glasses, they would probably cart you away to the nearest asylum. Unfortunately, for our society, in many cases, 98% of the population is wearing those glasses and the world, unfortunately, becomes the asylum.

I see a seven year old boy who is attending first grade for the second year and is having great difficulty attending in the classroom and learning to read. The teacher is exasperated and enraged, as was the previous teacher, and, like the previous teacher, is phoning the mother consistently and sending her notes to let her know that this child is intelligent enough to do the work and could do it *if he wanted to*. The mother, believing this myth—this lie that the teachers are perpetuating—is hitting the child, threatening him, taking away his Chanukah top to force him to do what he cannot do. The lie here that everyone is in agreement on is that this child wants to fail, is consciously and maliciously choosing to fail, and if they can punish him enough, he will change his mind and choose to succeed. This is a myth that runs rampant in our school system and that engenders misery, failure and hopelessness in numerous children and their parents.

Of course, the truth is totally other. No child or person *consciously* wants to and maliciously chooses to fail. This boy is a victim of his life and his circumstances and some organic abnormalities. His entire life has been a series of separations, deprivations and chaos. As a result,. he is terrified that, as he has lost every other important object in his life, he will lose his mother. Every sleeping and waking moment, he is obsessed by that fear. This fear is exaggerated by his own murderous wishes toward his mother and the subsequent fear of his being killed in retaliation for these wishes. Thus, this child lives with the constant terror of losing either himself or the only security he knows. It's hard to concentrate on reading when you need to worry about survival.

Throughout his life, this child has been given messages by his environment that he is no good, and, thus, he *unconsciously* lives to prove he is no good. He is also a victim of a minimal brain damage syndrome with attendant perceptual problems and attention deficit issues. And, if that were not enough, there was never enough order in his environment or one-to-one steady attention to teach him to sit and focus. With this multiplicity of problems running rampant in the small body, ignorant people say he could learn if he wants to.

This one boy will be helped. He is in therapy now; he is getting special tutoring and perceptual training at the New York Optometric Center and his therapist and a very knowledgeable and understanding principal are educating the mother and the teacher and providing him with speech therapy and resource facilities. He is doing gymnastics and karate for fun and to encourage him in those areas in which he is skilled and talented. In this one case, the glasses have been removed. The car has been realized to be a table and with the facts in place, a solution is possible. But how many are the instances in which the glasses are not removed? The table continues to be perceived as a car and the damage explodes into the individual soul and into the fiber of society.

On the other end of the spectrum is a sixty year old man— intelligent, attractive, well-functioning, whose wife has just left him after a twenty-five year marriage, who says that he feels wonderful and that three months after his wife's departure, he has found the woman of his dreams, a woman who understands him totally, appreciates him exactly as he is and is totally accepting and loving of his three children, including the autistic one. In the future, when this man is forced to remove his glasses—and he will—he will see that the separation panic and rage and hopelessness that he repressed with pills is still there, hasn't gone away and is acting-out in destructive fashion, that no person can honestly know another in two months, that no person can totally accept another and be wholly happy and sanguine about everything the other is or does and that no person can "love" three total strangers instantly or easily understand or know— never mind accept—the responsibility of caring for an autistic child. It is possible that this man has discovered a saint just recently descended from heaven. It is more likely that he has found a woman who is either lying to herself or to him because she knows herself so little, understands reality so little or wants a man so desperately. When the glasses come off, there will be horror ahead for all of them.

Myths, lies, lead only to misperception, misapprehension, ignorance, inability to solve problems productively, eventual damage and hurt in every direction. "The truth shall set them free" is not only a religious tenet but a psychological fact of the gravest proportions.

When we live by myth, often our best efforts are doomed to failure, and this repeated failure breeds in ourselves a sense of inadequacy, of "badness," "wrongness," valuelessness and hopelessness, self-hate and self-punishment. If you have been taught all your life that hard work and determination lead inevitably to success (a myth particularly unsuited to our society, where success is often the result of psychopathy), when you don't succeed, you assume that it's your fault, *you* haven't worked hard enough or been determined enough and you, then, don't feel very happy with yourself. If you have been taught all your life that if you are ethical and honest and decent, you will harvest the fruits of this world, and you don't, you will inevitably assume that you have not been adequately ethical, honest and decent and that there must be something morally wrong with you, otherwise why would all these bad things be happening to you (probably the reason for writing *When Bad Things Happen to Good People*), and you don't feel very good about yourself. If you have been taught all your life that positive thinking is what you need to do and you have negative thoughts and feelings that won't go away, then surely there must be something truly wrong with you. If you have been taught all your life that it's your job in life to please others, and, even when you twist your own self into a pretzel and try as hard as you know how, you're not pleasing others, surely that's your fault; there must be something wrong with you and you don't feel very good about yourself. If you have been taught all your life that people in families always love each other, always treat each other well, how can you understand that your thirteen year old yells that he hates you, your seven year old wishes that your thirteen year old were dead so that he could have his parents all to himself and you wish sometimes that your husband would be run over by the nearest vehicle? Surely you're a bad mother, and that fills you with shame and guilt and a sense of inadequacy and futility. If you have been taught all your life that a good person is a good citizen and a good citizen is one who fights for his country, and you can't register for the draft because killing a flea is abhorrent to you, then something severely wrong is operating in you and your "badness" and "wrongness" know no end.

In brief, living by myth, by lies which we cannot and should not, in reality, accommodate, leads to a mutilation of one's self-image into that of a despicable, hateful, worthless self. Anyone who has lived with this sense of self for any length of time, or anyone who knows intimately people with such a self-concept, or anyone who has worked clinically with this problem, knows the immense pain that these people feel in themselves, the immense damage that they do to themselves and those around them in their unconscious effort to express or deny this self-image and the multiple reverberations this problem has in the personal and the global. Indeed, a negative self-image is the heart and cornerstone of every emotional disorder.

The other great difficulty with the myths that permeate our world is that they are a contradiction in terms, offer double messages which are crazy-making and present to people, especially the developing child, a chaotic incoherent world where he feels unsafe because there is no coherent code to trust, no ordered world to understand and feel secure in, but contradictory truths that fight each other and make him feel like he's stuck in quicksand and doesn't know where to tread because he doesn't know where it will shift. The result is frustration, confusion, helplessness and a real terror for one's own survival.

Once in a consultation with a deeply depressed patient, he tentatively admitted that he thought he was going crazy. No, there were no hallucinations or hearing of voices. It was a much more subtle thing. All his life and even now, every day he remembered and experienced his mother telling him how much she loved him and how much she had always loved him and how much she would always love him. Yet, in all his life, he had never had a compliment from her or an affirmative statement. Although he was a good-looking, well-proportioned man, all she ever commented on was his big nose and the fact that he was too tall for most girls. When he achieved anything productive, she ignored it; when he came home crying about being beaten up by the neighborhood bullies, she not only did nothing about it but harassed him for being such a burden to her and making the family the neighborhood laughingstock. When his younger brother stole his money, she blamed him for having "left it around as a temptation." There was nothing that he could do or be that she could approve of, support, nurture, empathize with or accept. This man was in a state of great sadness and pain and helplessness. How, with all this love at his disposal, had he turned out so badly? How could he be repaying this woman so negatively for all her affection and concern?

What emerged, of course, is that his mother's "love" was a myth, a lie, because it was only half of the picture. Certainly, on some level his mother loved him. She cared for his physical being, she provided him with clothes, shelter, schooling; she spent time with him, etc. However, unbeknownst to both of them, for complicated reasons (inappropriate to address here), she also hated him and acted on this hatred. The words were of love; the many actions were of hatred. And, for the boy and the man, having lived with this central lie all his life, this partial contradictory message, he became so confused and helpless that he could no longer function in this world at all.

When, through therapy, he recognized the truth, understood its being and its sources and its outcomes, he was able to evaluate it and deal with the situation. He is now a fairly happy, functioning member of our society.

Just yesterday, a colleague called me, indignant and in shock. She had gone to a professional meeting where a group of therapists were to discuss cases and offer each other peer supervision and a relief from the isolation of the consulting room. Her shock concerned the personality and expertise of some of these therapists. One was so narcissistic that he had no realization that there was anyone else in the room. He spoke whenever he wanted to, interrupting whoever was speaking as if they literally did not exist, and on esoteric issues that had no relation to the matters at hand. He advocated medication for virtually every patient. Another therapist had totally misdiagnosed a situation and was addressing it with the patient in the worst possible manner. I had known this colleague for a long time and knew her to be a genuinely caring woman, a gifted therapist and a neutral, truthful observer. As I empathized with her distress, I believed her statements and observations totally. What surprised me was that this very intelligent and knowledgeable woman had somewhere internalized the myth that all therapists were honest, responsible, empathic, knowledgeable, etc.

So we think about doctors. Every one is a knight in a white lab coat, expert and caring, bound by the Hippocratic oath to treat us with skill, respect and dignity and to do the most that is possible for us to do. The truth is that therapists and doctors and lawyers are only people and, in a narcissistic culture, probably narcissistic people, self-involved and more concerned with their condos and their Mercedes than with us. When we understand the myths and don't accept them, then we'll look for the truth in each individual, find quality in those that have it and honor the right man rather than the imposed image.

A 32 year old woman had taken a job six months ago as a special resource room teacher at a local public school. A very dedicated woman who loved children and worked long and hard to do everything she could for them, she spent her nights crying. Her job, as her principal wanted her to practice it, was substantially different from the job description they had shown her when she was being interviewed. The budget for resource materials was half of what was promised. The assistant principal was taking credit for pupils' feats that the teacher was solely responsible for, and the principal and assistant principal had formed a power coalition to keep total control of everything and leave everyone else in the position of feudal vassals or unemployed. As we explored this very difficult situation, it became apparent that the difficulties rested not so much in the particular working situation. She loved her children. She loved her work. She knew that she was doing a great job and looked forward to her day. She was making a decent salary with decent benefits. She was not invested in outside honors or adulation. So what cause the nightly tears? The sadness and frustration and confusion and disappointment and fear were related to the contradictory messages this world was sending her. A deeply religious woman, from a small Southern town, she had been taught to think of people as trustworthy, honest, pleasant, cooperative, benign. She was taught that if she treated people well, they would treat her well; if she worked hard, she would be rewarded. What was she to make of this world where people lied, treated you badly, did not appreciate your good work, were surly and self-serving? How was she to behave? What was she to expect? What was the truth? What was reality? How was she to handle a reality that she didn't even know existed? Amidst her anguish, she was convinced that she was doing something wrong to cause this situation, that there was something greatly wrong with her, and she was terrified of what was going to happen next in her job and, by extension, in her world.

"Love thy neighbor as thyself," "Nice guys finish last," "Work hard and you'll get what you want," "Don't work hard, work smart,"

145

"This is the land of opportunity and equality for everyone," "The other half of America is starving" [John Kenneth Galbraith], "Ask not what your country can do for you, ask what you can do for your country," "Concentrate on number one," "We need a kinder, gentler society," "What's the bottom line?" Thousands of such contradictory myths and messages have filtered into our homes and into our society, and they have disoriented and confused and frustrated us and made us feel hopeless and impotent or, by extension, impulsive and acting-out. Who are we really? What should we do? What can we expect? How does our world function? What do we really believe? What should we believe? How should we function in it? We don't know. We don't have the answers but we don't admit to not having them so either we are ambivalent, terrified and don't make decisions lest we make a move that will cause the quicksand to shift and force us under, or we impulsively choose a course only to worry and feel guilty that we haven't chosen the other.

In his poem "The Road Not Taken," Robert Frost sets out for us the various possibilities of choice, the attractions and repulsions of each and the sadness and remorse and deprivation we feel at giving up one choice even though we approach with joy, curiosity and hope the choice we have made. What's lovely about this poem is not only the beauty of its language and structure, the empathy and reflection of our emotions, but the truth of the premise, the truth of how the world really functions—that for everything we have, there are things we have to give up.

Unlike Mr. Frost, the myths of our society lie to us. In their essence and in their contradiction of each other and in their persistence, either they teach us that we can have everything we want, that we don't have to give up anything, that there are no consequences to actions, or they confuse us so that we know not the truth of ourselves, of others, the human laws by which the world operates or what we need to do to be decent, effective people in a decent, effective society.

In the Woody Allen film *Another Woman*, the protagonist, in her mid-fifties, suddenly, through a series of coincidences and life situations, begins to discover the other woman in herself that she had never acknowledged. She recognizes that, in many ways, she had throughout her life lied to herself about who she was, what she was doing and what her relationships were about and she recognizes, with pain, how she has abused herself and others by the falsehoods she had perpetrated upon herself.

Dr. Scott Peck, in this book *People of the Lie*, gives us one devastating example after another of people who lie to themselves and bring disaster. He tells the painful story of a family where one of the sons had committed suicide and the other was so severely depressed that he was failing and his school had recommended counseling. Dr. Peck met with the couple—attractive, articulate, affluent, well-dressed and well-groomed. They refused to admit that there were any problems in the family, any problems with their parenting, any problems in the universe. They disregarded DR. Peck's recommendation for psychological evaluation of the boy and the second school's subsequent recommendation for treatment for the surviving son and sent him to a military school so that the "problem" could be hidden. In lying to themselves, in absolutely denying and avoiding the truth of facts and expert recommendation, they condemned one son to suicide and the other to suffering.

In the past several years, there have emerged in our society hundreds and thousands of accounts of the sexual abuse of young children. It is possible to have an abuse incident happen once, twice to a child and not know about it, but what about the cases of children who have regularly and systematically been abused for years? How is it that the other parent didn't "know"? How is it that they didn't see the personality changes in the child which always occur with instances of continual abuse? How did they account for the inappropriate time spent with the child, with the obvious problems in the couple's relationship? They account for it by lying, by wiping out and denying and avoiding the child's obvious distress and the other glaring information because they can't tolerate the pain and the struggle that would ensue from the truth. Thus, we lie and relegate our children to hell.

A former patient of mine had been regularly raped by her father from the ages of eight to fifteen. In those years, she gained seventy-five pounds and ballooned from a beautiful, graceful young girl to an obese, ungainly young woman. Her grades dropped so incredibly that she proceeded from a class for the gifted to a class for the learning disabled. She became a loner with no friends and no activities. When, at fifteen, she finally managed the courage to tell her mother, her mother flew into a rage, called her every possible unsavory name, insisted that she was a liar and insane and threw her out of the family. For a multitude of selfish reasons of her own, this mother could not face the truth, no matter in how many guises it presented itself and no matter in how many ways she condemned her daughter to disaster.

Another patient told of how in her Orthodox family her father had systematically and regularly raped every one of her five sisters, and the truth was never spoken or acknowledged by the mother or anyone in the family or in the Orthodox community where he was so highly regarded. Three of the daughters ended up in psychiatric wards of hospitals, one joined a cult and the last one is desperately trying to save herself.

Conversely, a supervisor of mine is seeing a seven year old girl who was abused by her mother's boyfriend. This mother recognized that her daughter's mood had changed, that she shrank in fear from the boyfriend's touch; speaking to her gently, openly and lovingly, she uncovered the truth. Immediately throwing the boyfriend out, she brought the child to therapy. After two years of treatment, the child has recovered her ebullient spirit, has become once again interested in her school and in her friends, has stopped having nightmares and is well on her way to a healthy future. In recognizing the truth, in refusing to lie to herself, in acknowledging information and using it to solve the problem, this mother has "saved" her daughter's emotional health, and probably her own.

This book is a plea for us to give up our madness, our myths, our clumsy lies about reality, individual and collective, and look the truth fearlessly in the face, for it is that that will be the start of our salvation. As Ernest Becker says, "The great characteristic of our time is that we know everything important about human nature that there is to know. Yet never has there been an age in which there is so much knowledge so securely possessed and yet so little is part of the common understanding." This is an attempt to make truth a part of our common understanding.

R.D. Lang in his book *Self and Other* delineates some characteristics of madness: "Ill people live in fantasy—imagine themselves, remake themselves in their fantasy image—remake their interactions with others . . ." "A schizophrenic is one who is confirmed in his false self and disconfirmed in his real self" [p. 84] . . . "Collusion is always clinched when self finds in the other one who will 'confirm' the self in the false self that the self is trying to make real" [p. 93] . . . "The technique of brainwashing is that of confusing or mystifying. This makes it difficult for the one person to know who he is or who the other is and what is the situation they are in. He does not know where he is anymore" [p. 123] . . . "When the issue is false and confused, the real or true conflict cannot come into focus. 'True' choices are not available and the person is in charge of psychosis."

The most critical element for madness—or crazy-making, as R.D. Lang describes it [p. 125]—is the double-bind situation. The 'victim' is caught in a triangle of paradoxical injunctions or attributions having the force of injunctions in which he cannot do the right thing. *The person does not know if he is coming or going.* The necessary ingredients for a double-bind situation are as follows: (1) Two or more persons. One of these is the victim. The double-bind is inflicted by mother alone or by some combination of mother, father and siblings. (2) Repeated experience so that the double-bind structure comes to be a habitual expectation. (3) A primary negative injunction—e.g., (a) "Do not do so-and-so or I will punish you," or (b) "If you do not do so-and-so, I will punish you." The first injunction is usually a verbal expression, e.g., "Come and kiss your loving mother." The secondary injunction is usually transmitted to the child by non-verbal means—posture, gesture, tone of voice, action, e.g., mother dropping her arms, turning rigid and not responding when the child comes to kiss her. In other words, double messages occur when the parent negates at some abstract level the injunction of the other.

"Those who deceive themselves are obliged to deceive others. It is impossible to maintain a false picture of myself unless I falsify your picture of yourself and me. I must disparage you if you are genuine, accuse you of being phony when you don't comply with what I want, say you are selfish if you get your own way, ridicule you for being immature if you try to be unselfish . . . the person caught in such a muddle does not know whether he is coming or going."

Perpetuating, disseminating, accepting lies or "myths," or "fantasies," acting lies by giving double messages, hearing lies or myths and not standing up to protect, living lies all give birth to madness. The only salvation practically, psychologically and spiritually is truth—that which is without secrecy, that which discloses itself without a veil, that which is genuine and not counterfeit. As Martin Buber proclaims, "Men need and it is granted

149

to them, to confirm one another in their individual being by means of *genuine* meetings; but beyond this they need and it is granted to them, to see the *truth*, which the soul gains by its struggle, light up the others, the brothers, in a different way, and even to be confirmed."

We must find a means for beaming the laser of truth on ourselves and our society so that we can somehow crawl out of this pit of myth and madness that we have created for ourselves.

About The Author

Miraim Kove began life as a Holocaust survivor. Perhaps, that has informed her life in her need to understand, expose and better the human condition. First, as an actress, then, as a teacher, than, as a mother and, for the last twenty-five years as a psychoanalytic psychotherapist, she has observed, explored, studied the individual and collective psyche. This book is an attempt to share some of these lessons learned in the hopes that they will illuminate issues that are facing us, to-day, as individuals, and, as a society and will point the way to possible productive, helpful solutions to our individual and societal dilemmas.